5/09

Field Guides to Find

Health Care

The Field Guides to Finding a New Career series

Advertising, Sales, and Marketing

Arts and Entertainment

Education

Film and Television

Food and Culinary Arts

Health Care

Information Technology

Internet and Media

Nonprofits and Government

Outdoor Careers

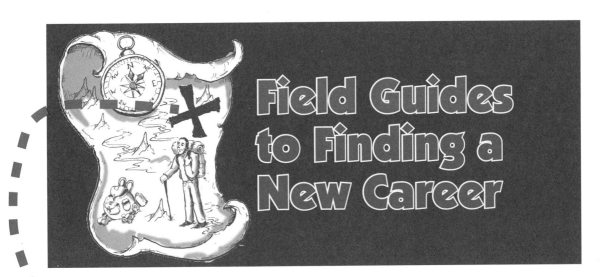

Field Guides
to Finding a
New Career

Health Care

By S. J. Stratford

Checkmark Books®
An imprint of Infobase Publishing

Field Guides to Finding a New Career: Health Care

Checkmark Books
An imprint of Infobase Publishing
132 West 31st Street
New York NY 10001

Library of Congress Cataloging-in-Publication Data

Stratford, S. J.
    Health care / by S. J. Stratford.
        p. cm. — (Field guide to finding a new career)
    Includes bibliographical references and index.
    ISBN-13: 978-0-8160-7600-0 (hardcover : alk. paper)
    ISBN-10: 0-8160-7600-6 (hardcover : alk. paper)
    ISBN-13: 978-0-8160-7624-6 (pbk. : alk. paper)
    ISBN-10: 0-8160-7624-3 (pbk. : alk. paper) 1. Allied health
personnel—Vocational guidance. I. Title.
    R697.A4S783 2009
    610.73'7069—dc22

                                        2008047834

Produced by Print Matters, Inc.
Text design by A Good Thing, Inc.
Illustrations by Molly Crabapple
Cover design by Takeshi Takahashi

Printed in the United States of America

Bang PMI 10 9 8 7 6 5 4 3 2 1

This book is printed on acid-free paper.

Contents

Introduction: Finding a New Career

Today, changing jobs is an accepted and normal part of life. In fact, according to the Bureau of Labor Statistics, Americans born between 1957 and 1964 held an average of 9.6 jobs from the ages of 18 to 36. The reasons for this are varied: To begin with, people live longer and healthier lives than they did in the past and accordingly have more years of active work life. However, the economy of the twenty-first century is in a state of constant and rapid change, and the workforce of the past does not always meet the needs of the future. Furthermore, fewer and fewer industries provide bonuses such as pensions and retirement health plans, which provide an incentive for staying with the same firm. Other workers experience epiphanies, spiritual growth, or various sorts of personal challenges that lead them to question the paths they have chosen.

Job instability is another prominent factor in the modern workplace. In the last five years, the United States has lost 2.6 *million jobs*; in 2005 alone, 370,000 workers were affected by mass layoffs. Moreover, because of new technology, changing labor markets, ageism, and a host of other factors, many educated, experienced professionals and skilled blue-collar workers have difficulty finding jobs in their former career tracks. Finally—and not just for women—the realities of juggling work and family life, coupled with economic necessity, often force radical revisions of career plans.

No matter how normal or accepted changing careers might be, however, the time of transition can also be a time of anxiety. Faced with the necessity of changing direction in the middle of their journey through life, many find themselves lost. Many career-changers find themselves asking questions such as: Where do I want to go from here? How do I get there? How do I prepare myself for the journey? Thankfully, the Field Guides to Finding a New Career are here to show the way. Using the language and visual style of a travel guide, we show you that reorienting yourself and reapplying your skills and knowledge to a new career is not an uphill slog, but an exciting journey of exploration. No matter whether you are in your twenties or close to retirement age, you can bravely set out to explore new paths and discover new vistas.

Though this series forms an organic whole, each volume is also designed to be a comprehensive, stand-alone, all-in-one guide to getting motivated, getting back on your feet, and getting back to work. We thoroughly discuss common issues such as going back to school, managing your household finances, putting your old skills to work in new situations, and selling yourself to potential employers. Each volume focuses on a broad career field, roughly grouped by Bureau of Labor Statistics' career clusters. Each chapter will focus on a particular career, suggesting new career paths suitable for an individual with that experience and training as well as practical issues involved in seeking and applying for a position.

Many times, the first question career-changers ask is, "Is this new path right for me?" Our self-assessment quiz, coupled with the career compasses at the beginning of each chapter, will help you to match your personal attributes to set you on the right track. Do you possess a storehouse of skilled knowledge? Are you the sort of person who puts others before yourself? Are you methodical and organized? Do you communicate effectively and clearly? Are you good at math? And how do you react to stress? All of these qualities contribute to career success—but they are not equally important in all jobs.

Many career-changers find working for themselves to be more hassle-free and rewarding than working for someone else. However, going at it alone, whether as a self-employed individual or a small-business owner, provides its own special set of challenges. Appendix A, "Going Solo: Starting Your Own Business," is designed to provide answers to many common questions and solutions to everyday problems, from income taxes to accounting to providing health insurance for yourself and your family.

For those who choose to work for someone else, how do you find a job, particularly when you have been out of the labor market for a while? Appendix B, "Outfitting Yourself for Career Success," is designed to answer these questions. It provides not only advice on résumé and self-presentation, but also the latest developments in looking for jobs, such as online resources, headhunters, and placement agencies. Additionally, it recommends how to explain an absence from the workforce to a potential employer.

Changing careers can be stressful, but it can also be a time of exciting personal growth and discovery. We hope that the Field Guides to Finding a New Career not only help you get your bearings in today's employment jungle, but set you on the path to personal fulfillment, happiness, and prosperity.

How to Use This Book

Career Compasses

Each chapter begins with a series of "career compasses" to help you get your bearings and determine if this job is right for you, based on your answers to the self-assessment quiz at the beginning of the book. Does it require a mathematical mindset? Communication skills? Organizational skills? If you're not a "people person," a job requiring you to interact with the public might not be right for you. On the other hand, your organizational skills might be just what are needed in the back office.

Destination

A brief overview, giving you an introduction to the career, briefly explaining what it is, its advantages, why it is so satisfying, its growth potential, and its income potential.

You Are Here

A self-assessment asking you to locate yourself on your journey. Are you working in a related field? Are you working in a field where some skills will transfer? Or are you doing something completely different? In each case, we suggest ways to reapply your skills, gain new ones, and launch yourself on your new career path.

Navigating the Terrain

To help you on your way, we have provided a handy map showing the stages in your journey to a new career. "Navigating the Terrain" will show you the road you need to follow to get where you are going. Since the answers are not the same for everyone and every career, we are sure to show how there are multiple ways to get to the same destination.

Organizing Your Expedition

Fleshing out "Navigating the Terrain," we give explicit directions on how to enter this new career: Decide on a destination, scout the terrain, and decide on a path that is right for you. Of course, the answers are not the same for everyone.

Landmarks

People have different needs at different ages. "Landmarks" presents advice specific to the concerns of each age demographic: early career (twenties), mid-career (thirties to forties), senior employees (fifties) and second-career starters (sixties). We address not only issues such as overcoming age discrimination, but also possible concerns of spouses and families (for instance, paying college tuition with reduced income) and keeping up with new technologies.

Essential Gear

Indispensable tips for career-changers on things such as gearing your résumé to a job in a new field, finding contacts and networking, obtaining further education and training, and how to gain experience in the new field.

Notes from the Field

Sometimes it is useful to consult with those who have gone before for insights and advice. "Notes from the Field" presents interviews with career-changers, presenting motivations and methods that you can identify with.

Further Resources

Finally, we give a list of "expedition outfitters" to provide you with further information and trade resources.

Make the Most of Your Journey

For someone interested in science and being a help to people or animals, health care is a natural fit. The profession has always attracted dynamic, passionate people who are excited about the possibility to do good in the world and see real progress in individuals. Medicine is as much about the heart as the head, so although you may be whip-smart in all the relevant scientific disciplines for your interest, you must also have genuine compassion for people and their well-being.

Health care is exciting because it is a constantly growing field. While this book includes common, established professions such as nursing and pharmacy, the bulk of the careers discussed are comparatively new. Even complementary and alternative medicine, which in many cases is based on ancient practices and knowledge, is only recently becoming widely popular among the public and gaining acceptance in the general health care community. Jobs that combine a variety of skills, such as nurse practitioner and physician assistant, are growing so quickly that there are not enough qualified candidates to fill the positions, according to the U.S. Bureau of Labor Statistics.

Professions that are devoted to a specific kind of assistance, such as physical and occupational therapy, are also on the rise. Medical advances mean that people are living longer, surviving horrific injuries that once would have been fatal, or surviving premature birth. All these people can live healthy, full, productive lives, but they may need some extra, specific assistance and so targeted therapists are required to help people overcome either physical or mental injuries or disabilities and achieve their full potential.

Medical advances have also given rise to professions like genetic counselors. As more and more is understood about genetics, more tests are available and the possibility of inherited disorders or diseases can be identified. A genetic counselor works intimately with families to discuss findings and options ranging from prenatal decisions to geriatric concerns.

Another common thread in the career choices discussed in this book is that nearly all of them allow a professional to spend more time and give more hands-on care to a patient than an allopath (a physician who practices conventional medicine) is able to in today's medical world.

Many qualified students are turned off by traditional routes in medical school and by the restrictions and heavy costs imposed on doctors by insurance companies. The administrative politics of being a health professional can make the job more about dealing with paperwork than helping people. Doctors are frustrated by short appointment times and heavy schedules. Limitations in insurance mean that patients cannot get the full breadth of care they need. People who enter the field wanting to be a real help to society find themselves often overwhelmed by the unfortunate realities of the modern American medical world.

However, potential heath care professionals can still be exhilarated by the opportunity to make a difference in patient lives. A physical therapist combines his or her scientific aptitude with a desire to help people and gets to work one-to-one with a patient, seeing real results over a period of time. A nurse practitioner may get deeply involved in a community, often filling the role that once was filled by a neighborhood doctor. Likewise, people often have a closer relationship with their pharmacist than their doctor—the pharmacist will give patients more detailed information and advice about their medication than the doctor has time for.

As research has shown the efficacy of more natural techniques in healing, caring physicians have been incorporating alternative medicine into their practices. Natural alternative healing is often less invasive to the patient, and often reduces the need to prescribe an abundance of chemical-based medications. Professions like osteopathy and chiropractic medicine allow someone with a strong science background and an interest in alternative forms of healing to combine the two, using a variety of techniques to overcome pain or a chronic condition that would once have required surgery or complex pain management techniques. Properly accredited schools of chiropractic medicine, osteopathy, and alternative medicine teach students standard procedures and give them credentials so they can begin practicing. The fields are constantly evolving, and a clever, interested practitioner can certainly be an integral part of that evolution.

A word about accreditation—every profession discussed in this book requires the completion of an accredited program to earn a degree or certificate. To be accredited, a school or program must meet certain set standards and requirements as established by a national governing board, often in tandem with the U.S. Department of Education. Accredited programs in every field can be found easily using the Internet.

Because so many of the professions are comparatively new, there may not be many accredited programs in the country. If you do not have the option of moving to attend school, this can be a problem. National associations representing your chosen field will be able to advise you. There may be a school in your area that is a candidate for accreditation, for example, or distance learning might be an option. Attending an accredited school is a must, even in the areas of complementary and alternative medicine. Without accreditation, you have no way of ascertaining whether the program is truly reputable. Furthermore, you may find that if you attend a non-accredited program, you will have a harder time gaining employment or making advancements. If you take the work of health care seriously, you must also take yourself seriously as a student. This means that you must make the extra effort to research and apply to an accredited school so that you can feel confident you are getting the best education possible.

The passion you have for helping people and affecting positive change in society is also important because it will offer you greater compensation than you might reap financially. While most of the professions discussed in this book will offer decent wages, these are not the medical professions to pursue if you wish to become rich. With the exception of veterinary technicians, you stand to earn a mid-range salary with the bulk of these jobs, although some, such as pharmacists, osteopaths, and certain complementary medicine professionals, will pay substantive salaries. No matter which health care path you choose, grants, fellowships, work-study, and low-interest loans are often available to help pay for your education. Because the need is so great for capable nurse practitioners and physician assistants, schools often offer tuition reimbursement to those pursuing these careers, and additional financial support may be available to those who make a commitment to work in high-need areas, such as depressed inner cities or rural communities.

Along those lines, you will see that a number of the health care professions in this book suggest that you be bilingual and well-versed in a variety of cultures and traditions. Part of being a real asset to the community you wish to serve, and a hands-on provider of health, is being able to truly communicate with your patients. While not having language skills should certainly never prevent you from pursuing any of these careers, you should at least consider trying to learn a language like Spanish because it will enhance your credentials and employment options.

You may also work with people from a wide range of socioeconomic and cultural and educational backgrounds. The more you understand about such communities, including their traditional approaches to health care, diet, exercise, and general wellness, the more effective you can be in helping them achieve and maintain optimum health. A better understanding of where patients are coming from and what their day-to-day realities are vis-à-vis diet and exercise—be they constricted by finances, time, or a cultural tradition that precludes certain activities—will help you truly assist your patients.

A big part of modern medicine is being adaptive. You have to be open to your patients' needs and willing and able to make changes to standard practice based upon those needs. The unexpected will always arise and you have to be someone who can handle it with aplomb and even enthusiasm. You have to understand that the "tried and true" often is not, or is not anymore, and you may need to work a little harder and think a little differently to find an option that works.

Finally, while all these professions require a certain amount of schooling, you should embrace the reality that you will never stop learning. Many professions require you to take a certain number of continuing education courses each year in order to remain certified. Furthermore, with every aspect of medicine constantly growing and changing, there is always going to be something new to learn. Much of being a successful health care provider is about asking questions—of your patients, of your profession, and of yourself. If you are someone who is endlessly inquisitive, always eager to expand your knowledge and mind, and truly wants to be an active, involved giver in society, you should not hesitate to pursue a career in health care.

Self-Assessment Quiz

I: Relevant Knowledge

1. How many years of specialized training have you had?
   (a) None, it is not required
   (b) Several weeks to several months of training
   (c) A year-long course or other preparation
   (d) Years of preparation in graduate or professional school, or equivalent job experience

2. Would you consider training to obtain certification or other required credentials?
   (a) No
   (b) Yes, but only if it is legally mandated
   (c) Yes, but only if it is the industry standard
   (d) Yes, if it is helpful (even if not mandatory)

3. In terms of achieving success, how would rate the following qualities in order from least to most important?
   (a) ability, effort, preparation
   (b) ability, preparation, effort
   (c) preparation, ability, effort
   (d) preparation, effort, ability

4. How would you feel about keeping track of current developments in your field?
   (a) I prefer a field where very little changes
   (b) If there were a trade publication, I would like to keep current with that
   (c) I would be willing to regularly recertify my credentials or learn new systems
   (d) I would be willing to aggressively keep myself up-to-date in a field that changes constantly

5. For whatever reason, you have to train a bright young successor to do your job. How quickly will he or she pick it up?
   (a) Very quickly
   (b) He or she can pick up the necessary skills on the job
   (c) With the necessary training he or she should succeed with hard work and concentration
   (d) There is going to be a long breaking-in period—there is no substitute for experience

II: Caring

1. How would you react to the following statement: "Other people are the most important thing in the world?"
   (a) No! Me first!
   (b) I do not really like other people, but I do make time for them
   (c) Yes, but you have to look out for yourself first
   (d) Yes, to such a degree that I often neglect my own well-being

2. Who of the following is the best role model?
   (a) Ayn Rand
   (b) Napoléon Bonaparte
   (c) Bill Gates
   (d) Florence Nightingale

3. How do you feel about pets?
   (a) I do not like animals at all
   (b) Dogs and cats and such are OK, but not for me
   (c) I have a pet, or I wish I did
   (d) I have several pets, and caring for them occupies significant amounts of my time

4. Which of the following sets of professions seems most appealing to you?
   (a) business leader, lawyer, entrepreneur
   (b) politician, police officer, athletic coach
   (c) teacher, religious leader, counselor
   (d) nurse, firefighter, paramedic

5. How well would you have to know someone to give them $100 in a harsh but not life-threatening circumstance? It would have to be...
    (a) ...a close family member or friend (brother or sister, best friend)
    (b) ...a more distant friend or relation (second cousin, coworkers)
    (c) ...an acquaintance (a coworker, someone from a community organization or church)
    (d) ...a complete stranger

III: Organizational Skills

1. Do you create sub-folders to further categorize the items in your "Pictures" and "Documents" folders on your computer?
    (a) No
    (b) Yes, but I do not use them consistently
    (c) Yes, and I use them consistently
    (d) Yes, and I also do so with my e-mail and music library

2. How do you keep track of your personal finances?
    (a) I do not, and I am never quite sure how much money is in my checking account
    (b) I do not really, but I always check my online banking to make sure I have money
    (c) I am generally very good about budgeting and keeping track of my expenses, but sometimes I make mistakes
    (d) I do things such as meticulously balance my checkbook, fill out Excel spreadsheets of my monthly expenses, and file my receipts

3. Do you systematically order commonly used items in your kitchen?
    (a) My kitchen is a mess
    (b) I can generally find things when I need them
    (c) A place for everything, and everything in its place
    (d) Yes, I rigorously order my kitchen and do things like alphabetize spices and herbal teas

4. How do you do your laundry?
    (a) I cram it in any old way
    (b) I separate whites and colors

    (c)   I separate whites and colors, plus whether it gets dried

    (d)   Not only do I separate whites and colors and drying or non-drying, I organize things by type of clothes or some other system

5. Can you work in clutter?

    (a)   Yes, in fact I feel energized by the mess

    (b)   A little clutter never hurt anyone

    (c)   No, it drives me insane

    (d)   Not only does my workspace need to be neat, so does that of everyone around me

IV: Communication Skills

1. Do people ask you to speak up, not mumble, or repeat yourself?

    (a)   All the time

    (b)   Often

    (c)   Sometimes

    (d)   Never

2. How do you feel about speaking in public?

    (a)   It terrifies me

    (b)   I can give a speech or presentation if I have to, but it is awkward

    (c)   No problem!

    (d)   I frequently give lectures and addresses, and I am very good at it

3. What's the difference between *their, they're,* and *there*?

    (a)   I do not know

    (b)   I know there is a difference, but I make mistakes in usage

    (c)   I know the difference, but I can not articulate it

    (d)   *Their* is the third-person possessive, *they're* is a contraction for *they are,* and *there* is a deictic adverb meaning "in that place"

4. Do you avoid writing long letters or e-mails because you are ashamed of your spelling, punctuation, and grammatical mistakes?

    (a)   Yes

    (b)   Yes, but I am either trying to improve or just do not care what people think

(c) The few mistakes I make are easily overlooked

(d) Save for the occasional typo, I do not ever make mistakes in usage

5. Which choice best characterizes the most challenging book you are willing to read in your spare time?
    (a) I do not read
    (b) Light fiction reading such as the Harry Potter series, *The Da Vinci Code*, or mass-market paperbacks
    (c) Literary fiction or mass-market nonfiction such as history or biography
    (d) Long treatises on technical, academic, or scientific subjects

V: Mathematical Skills

1. Do spreadsheets make you nervous?
    (a) Yes, and I do not use them at all
    (b) I can perform some simple tasks, but I feel that I should leave them to people who are better-qualified than myself
    (c) I feel that I am a better-than-average spreadsheet user
    (d) My job requires that I be very proficient with them

2. What is the highest level math class you have ever taken?
    (a) I flunked high-school algebra
    (b) Trigonometry or pre-calculus
    (c) College calculus or statistics
    (d) Advanced college mathematics

3. Would you rather make a presentation in words or using numbers and figures?
    (a) Definitely in words
    (b) In words, but I could throw in some simple figures and statistics if I had to
    (c) I could strike a balance between the two
    (d) Using numbers as much as possible; they are much more precise

4. Cover the answers below with a sheet of paper, and then solve the following word problem: Mary has been legally able to vote for exactly half her life. Her husband John is three years older than she. Next year,

their son Harvey will be exactly one-quarter of John's age. How old was Mary when Harvey was born?
(a) I couldn't work out the answer
(b) 25
(c) 26
(d) 27

5. Cover the answers below with a sheet of paper, and then solve the following word problem: There are seven children on a school bus. Each child has seven book bags. Each bag has seven big cats in it. Each cat has seven kittens. How many legs are there on the bus?
   (a) I couldn't work out the answer
   (b) 2,415
   (c) 16,821
   (d) 10,990

VI: Ability to Manage Stress

1. It is the end of the working day, you have 20 minutes to finish an hour-long job, and you are scheduled to pick up your children. Your supervisor asks you why you are not finished. You:
   (a) Have a panic attack
   (b) Frantically redouble your efforts
   (c) Calmly tell her you need more time, make arrangements to have someone else pick up the kids, and work on the project past closing time
   (d) Calmly tell her that you need more time to do it right and that you have to leave, or ask if you can release this flawed version tonight

2. When you are stressed, do you tend to:
   (a) Feel helpless, develop tightness in your chest, break out in cold sweats, or have other extreme, debilitating physiological symptoms?
   (b) Get irritable and develop a hair-trigger temper, drink too much, obsess over the problem, or exhibit other "normal" signs of stress?
   (c) Try to relax, keep your cool, and act as if there is no problem
   (d) Take deep, cleansing breaths and actively try to overcome the feelings of stress

3. The last time I was so angry or frazzled that I lost my composure was:
   (a) Last week or more recently
   (b) Last month
   (c) Over a year ago
   (d) So long ago I cannot remember

4. Which of the following describes you?
   (a) Stress is a major disruption in my life, people have spoken to me about my anger management issues, or I am on medication for my anxiety and stress
   (b) I get anxious and stressed out easily
   (c) Sometimes life can be a challenge, but you have to climb that mountain!
   (d) I am generally easygoing

5. What is your ideal vacation?
   (a) I do not take vacations; I feel my work life is too demanding
   (b) I would just like to be alone, with no one bothering me
   (c) I would like to do something not too demanding, like a cruise, with friends and family
   (d) I am an adventurer; I want to do exciting (or even dangerous) things and visit foreign lands

Scoring:

For each category...

For every answer of *a*, add zero points to your score.
For every answer of *b*, add ten points to your score.
For every answer of *c*, add fifteen points to your score.
For every answer of *d*, add twenty points to your score.

The result is your percentage in that category.

Nurse

Nurse

Career Compasses

Guide yourself to a career as a registered nurse.

Relevant Knowledge of all aspects of your given specialty, including sources for new information (25%)

Caring about the patient and everything related to your specific area of expertise (30%)

Communication Skills to work effectively with patients, family members, and the doctor managing the case, or to educate the general public (20%)

Organizational Skills to maintain charts and keep a unit or department running smoothly (25%)

Destination: Nurse

From Florence Nightingale, Clara Barton, and Margaret Sanger to any number of fictional depictions in books, film, and television, the ideal of the nurse is of a caring, devoted, and usually female person who gives her all to the needs of her patient. The modern world of nursing is still majority female, but it is a profession that actively seeks anyone who is smart and truly caring and actively interested in doing good for people at various stages of health.

At about 2.5 million jobs, registered nurses (RNs) comprise the largest group in the health care umbrella, and the demand for quality RNs is only growing. RNs are involved not only in treating patients but in educating patients, family, and the general public about medical conditions and home treatments. It is usually the nurse, rather than the doctor overseeing a given case, who offers the bulk of advice and emotional support to the family when dealing with an illness or injury. When a patient arrives at the hospital, a nurse takes his or her medical history, notes symptoms, conducts some preliminary diagnostic tests, and evaluates the results. Throughout the course of a shift, a nurse also monitors and operates some medical equipment and administers medication and certain treatments. The nurse remains on board for patient follow-up and rehabilitation.

Many nurses are involved in health education and community outreach. They work one-to-one with patients and family members to be sure they understand the home treatment program and nutritional and exercise requirements. The nurse also teaches a patient or family member how to administer medication, whether via injection—as with diabetes—or oral dosage. Nurses work with new parents to be sure they understand all the immediate basics including healthy diapering, feeding, swaddling, and sleep habits. For wider community education, nurses are involved in public health screenings, immunization clinics, blood drives, and seminars on current topics of health concern.

Far from just taking temperatures, nurses work closely with doctors when a patient is in the hospital, monitoring their condition, setting up and maintaining an IV, administering medicine, and discussing progress. Nurses with the proper advanced education may even write prescriptions.

Nearly 60 percent of nurses work in hospitals. Many of them choose to specialize in a particular area of care. There are four general options in specializing. Nurses can choose to become a perioperative nurse, for example, which means assisting in the operation room. Or they might focus on a specific health concern such as diabetes or cancer. Another option is to work with organs or body system concerns, such as dermatology, a rapidly growing field. Or they may focus on a specific patient group, as with pediatric nurses, who work with children. They can, of course, combine focuses, as with pediatric nurses who work with children who have specific conditions or diseases.

Additionally, there are critical care nurses, who work in the intensive or critical care units with patients needing close attention and complex treatment. Emergency nurses, as seen on *ER*, specialize in trauma and perform quick initial assessments and care. They can also gain the qualification to work as transport nurses, traveling with a patient via air. A hospice, or palliative care, nurse works in a nursing home or hospice, where the focus is on keeping a patient comfortable during a long terminal illness.

Home care nurses are also very much in demand as the population ages but many elderly are still functional enough not to need to relocate to a group home. A home care nurse can work either temporarily or long-term, depending on a patient's need. They either take up residence in the home or stay from morning till evening, providing therapy and medication as needed.

Essential Gear

Small laptop or PDA. Medicine changes frequently, requiring regular updating of medical and pharmacological books. A nurse engaged in administering medication might prefer to keep the latest information on a personal computer or PDA. This is efficient and expedient, and in these days of heavy patient loads, anything that can speed something up is welcome.

Other specialized careers include ambulatory nurse, holistic nurse, long-term care nurse, medical-surgical nurse, occupational health nurse, perianesthesia nurse, psychiatric-mental health nurse, radiology nurses, rehabilitation nurse, and transplant nurse. Whatever your particular interest in medicine may be, you can find an area that is right for you.

While the bulk of nurses work in hospitals or other health care organizations, many find employment in private offices and schools as well as homes. The job can be taxing—nurses often talk about being on their feet most of the day. Working with people with serious, contagious diseases or unpredictable mental disorders can also pose hazards to health and well-being, but nurses take necessary precautions. And while hospitals and nurses' unions have worked to try and make shifts more reasonable, they often last for 12 hours, and a nurse must be prepared to work nights, weekends, and holidays, as well as be on call.

The training to become a nurse is less arduous and expensive than that for becoming a doctor, but it is still involved. Three educational routes are available: a bachelor's of science degree in nursing, associate's degree in nursing, or diploma from an accredited nursing program, although the first two are the most common. After completing an educational program a nurse must then pass a national licensing exam to gain the license and begin practice. Continuing education may be needed depending upon the area of specialty chosen, and of course nurses should take more classes regularly to keep up with medical changes and advances. Further education can also lead to wider work opportunities.

For those who have a degree and are looking to move into nursing, accelerated programs are available. You can also obtain a master's degree in nursing, if you have a comparable degree in another field. Although the cost of the education may be a concern at any level, many programs offer some form of tuition reimbursement. A bachelor's of science in nursing (BSN) or master's of science in nursing (MSN) may prove to be worth the extra time and money spent because upon completion you automatically have a wider range of opportunities in both work and salary.

Whether you have been involved in some form of health care work already and want to advance or are needing a radical change and want to feel more connected to the community, you should consider what area of nursing might suit you and be prepared for an exciting, challenging, and satisfying journey.

You Are Here

Determine if you have the skills and temperament for nursing.

Do you have strong, personal dedication? While you can complete the educational requirements and even secure a job, you will be neither happy nor truly successful as a nurse if you are not someone who can dedicate yourself wholeheartedly to patient care and the regular promotion of good health among the population as a whole. Nursing is often considered not as well paid as it should be for the type of work that is involved. Whether you find this to be the case or not is fairly immaterial—what matters is that you are someone who will pay attention to and give the utmost care to all your patients. This may sound like a given, but bear in mind that many patients can be difficult or even abusive. You have to be someone who can handle that and still do your job.

Do you have a lot of stamina? In addition to all the standing and walking, nurses bend, stretch, support the full weight of a patient, and otherwise strain themselves throughout the course of a shift. They must also remain alert to monitor equipment, dosages, charts, and graphs. They provide whatever care and therapy is needed to what may be as many as 10 patients or even more. They also have to be ready to act on a moment's notice if a patient has a serious setback, which involves a lot of detailed work at top speed. Many hospital nurses are engaged in strenuous work, and you have to be prepared to handle it.

Are you well-organized with an excellent memory? In a hospital, or any health care facility, charts and computerized information are available on every patient. However, a nurse needs to be sharp and remember who gets what care and what might be required for any given patient. When taking histories, a nurse may be interrupted several times during the proceedings. During a shift, any number of issues can come up all at once, and there is not time to check the chart. A nurse who can balance all this, dovetail, and keep pertinent information in mind will do very well.

Navigating the Terrain

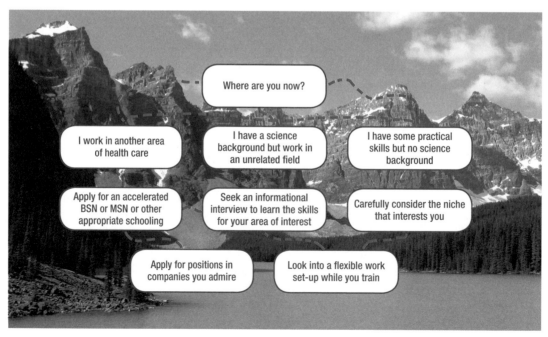

Where are you now?

I work in another area of health care

I have a science background but work in an unrelated field

I have some practical skills but no science background

Apply for an accelerated BSN or MSN or other appropriate schooling

Seek an informational interview to learn the skills for your area of interest

Carefully consider the niche that interests you

Apply for positions in companies you admire

Look into a flexible work set-up while you train

Organizing Your Expedition

Gather your tongue depressors and start down the road toward nursing.

Determine your area of specialty. With a myriad of possibilities to choose from, people who want to be involved with helping others have some serious decisions to make as they get into their degree work. Of course, you can always change your focus, or narrow your approach as you get nearer completion of your degree, but it really helps to have a good sense of what sort of area you want to pursue. Take into consideration your skills, knowledge base, abilities, and interests. Also factor in your personality. Oncological nurses see many of their cancer patients suffer and many die. While the continuing improvements in cancer screenings and treatments are encouraging, the nurse still deals with a lot of patient difficulty and tragedy. You not only have to be up on the latest chemotherapy dosages and contraindications, you have to be able to deal with very ill people and their distraught friends and families every day. Some people take to this very naturally, whereas others simply cannot handle it. Whatever area you are drawn to, ask a hospital or care facility if you might be allowed to observe the routine, or otherwise get some practical information to help you plan your program and future.

Essential Gear

Arch-supporting shoes. Nurses' shoes are an old joke, but the reality is that you do want to invest in a few pairs of really well-made and comfortable shoes. Clogs, which offer strong arch supports, are some of nurses' favorites. You need something wide and breathable that will promote good posture, especially when you are on your feet for 12 hours straight.

Research your degree program. Where you go to school will probably not affect where you end up working, but if there is somewhere specific you wish to be—say, for example, that you have a young family and uprooting them would be difficult—you should investigate teaching hospitals or programs that might have a degree-to-work aspect. You should certainly talk to an advisor before you begin. They may be able to tell you about job prospects in your location. He or she should certainly be able to tell you what sort of specialty might best guarantee a job in your

Notes from the Field

Tom Tente
Registered nurse, Baystate Medical Center ER
Easthampton, Massachusetts

What were you doing before you decided to become a registered nurse?

I had a BS in health sciences from Boston University. I was working as a tech in exercise testing at Beth Israel hospital for a couple of years, and during that time I got to work with a lot of registered nurses. I was totally impressed with their work—the care they gave, as well as their knowledge and expertise.

Why did you decide to pursue a career as a registered nurse?

In addition to being inspired by the nurses whose work I was getting to observe daily, I wanted to do more with my own work. I was feeling frustrated by my job and hungry for something more challenging and satisfying. I felt that nursing would give me more options, allow me to change fields, put me in a position where I could gain more respect, and of course allow me to make more money. I felt that combining an RN degree with exercise testing would complement each other quite well.

What was involved in terms of education and training?

I went back to Boston University to get my RN degree, because it was an 18-month program and as an alumnus, I could get in immediately,

chosen town. Furthermore, you want to look at the school's record. Do they have a strong reputation? Do most of their graduates go on to good jobs? These are all things you should know before you apply.

Decide if you prefer administration or hands-on care. A registered nurse does not necessarily have to be personally engaged with patients. You could be a case manager, an infection control nurse, an educator, administrator, consultant, pharmaceutical researcher, or medical editor or writer. The various possibilities may help you choose a path if you have a strong background in a related field. A former lawyer might look into becoming a legal nurse consultant, for example, which involves assisting with medical legal cases doing interviewing, reviewing and organizing medical records, and advising lawyers on medical issues. Someone who *whereas if I hoped to go to the University of Massachusetts, I would have to wait a whole year—and I didn't want to wait. When you know what you want to do, you want to get started right away. Besides, the longer I would have to wait, the more likely it was that I would have to retake some of the courses I'd taken from my original degree because of new developments in the field. This way, I could get into a hospital sooner and keep up with changes while on the job. Of course, the big disadvantage to going back to BU was that tuition was about twice as much as that of U Mass, but it was worth it.*

What are the keys to success and qualities that make a good registered nurse?

Don't be afraid to ask questions! That is a way to both advocate for your patient and also to learn. Also, you have to be able to multitask. There is an incredible amount of daily distractions, so you need to be flexible and stay focused. I also believe that change is good. In nursing, you can change jobs to develop new skills and even try a totally different specialty. You can really grow professionally by expanding your knowledge that way. It really helps to have a background in physiology—that made a big difference for me. A lot of people don't realize how much of nursing requires it, especially in critical care settings.

has worked in another care-providing arena, such as with abuse victims, might consider forensics nursing, which entails assisting in forensics investigation, often relating to violent crime. Anyone with a background in teaching might find a whole new joy in educating both health care workers and the public in general, and someone interested in politics can find advocacy work in improving access to health care.

Landmarks

If you are in your twenties . . . You should take your time researching to find a specialty. Before applying for school, look for volunteer opportunities or internships. This way, you will be able to observe the work firsthand and gain both knowledge and practical experience before you begin your formal education.

If you are in your thirties or forties . . . Consider how your present job or skills and knowledge base could best translate to some aspect of nursing. This age group can be considered ideal for nursing, as they are perceived as steadier and more stable than a younger group. When you determine your course, you will likely have no trouble getting work.

If you are in your fifties . . . Look for a program that easily transitions from whatever you have already been doing. If you have been a home-maker caring for children, pediatrics is an obvious route. If you have experience managing a busy, detail-oriented office, you might look into administration.

If you are over sixty . . . Look for an aspect of nursing that is not overly strenuous. You may be a natural fit for a private doctor's office, or an assistant to an occupational therapist or something similar. Likewise, you should look into home health care. Many elderly patients feel more comfortable being looked after by someone in your age range.

Further Resources

American Nurses Association A membership organization that works to promote the profession, nurses' rights, lobby Congress on issues and provide individual assistance to members with a job board and other information. http://nursingworld.org

American Association of Colleges of Nursing The AACN establishes standards of excellence for educational programs and helps administrators implement those standards. It is a useful source to contact when choosing schools. You also want to be sure your chosen program has received AACN accreditation. http://www.aacn.nche.edu

National Student Nurses' Association Providing job opportunities, live chat, assorted publications and other member benefits, the NSNA is invaluable to anyone currently earning his or her degree in nursing. http://www.nsna.org

Nurse Practitioner

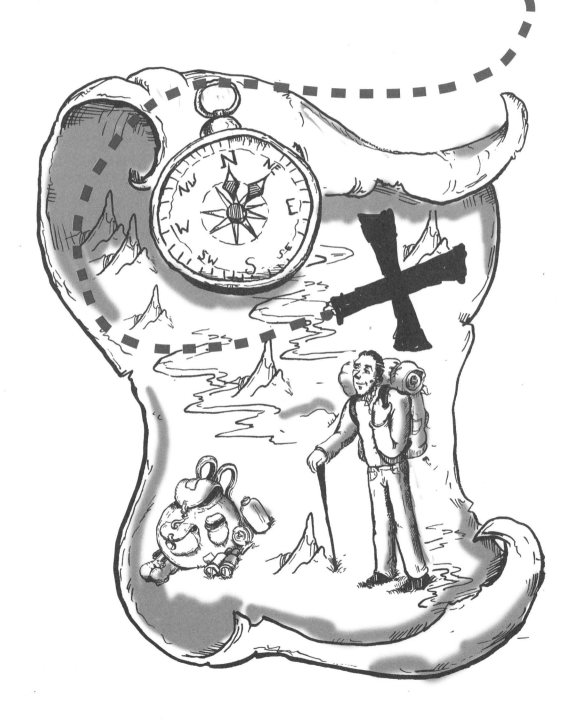

Nurse Practitoner

Career Compasses

Guide yourself to a career as a nurse practitioner.

Relevant Knowledge of your specialty and the community in which you are serving (20%)

Caring about your patient load and the community at large (30%)

Communication Skills to work effectively with patients, family members, and other caregivers and medical professionals (25%)

Organizational Skills to maintain patient records, keep track of changes in pertinent governmental programs, and balance patient and administrative needs (25%)

Destination: Nurse Practitioner

A nurse practitioner (NP) is a registered nurse who has completed a further degree and been trained to diagnose and manage a number of medical conditions and illnesses. An NP is licensed to provide primary and specialty care, which usually involves a mix of nursing and other health care services. They usually work in such areas as family practice, adult care, women's health, pediatrics, acute care, and geriatrics, although they also work in neonatology (a pediatric subspecialty dealing with the medical care of newborn infants) and mental health. They can also write prescriptions. While NPs work closely with doctors, they provide enough of the same care that many patients in reasonable health have a nurse practitioner as their sole health care provider, rather than a licensed allopath.

Nurse practitioning is all about individualized care. The focus is on the patient and their condition and the promotion of overall wellness, rather than invasive treatment and medication. The whole of a patient's life and needs are taken into consideration when evaluating a medical condition, and more time is spent in thought and the development of a program than in most standard medical practice. The priorities are on prevention and education, and patients are encouraged to take an active interest in their health and treatment choices. Many nurse practitioners are also involved with research and patient advocacy.

The actual day-to-day work varies depending on your location because nurse practitioners are subject to regulations by the state. This is something to bear in mind if you want to move—you will have to take a state examination to procure a new license, and you may need to move into a different specialty as well. The requirements from state to state are fairly basic, and nursing organizations can assist and advise you.

Overall, an NP's job entails patient education and counseling; collaboration with other health providers, including referrals; the diagnosis and treatment of acute illnesses, infections, and injuries; the diagnosis, treatment, and monitoring of chronic illnesses; performing exams; performing and analyzing diagnostic tests; writing prescriptions; advising on and prescribing rehabilitation treatments; providing basic family care from prenatal to childhood immunizations, to adult health maintenance.

Since nurse practitioners can provide health services similar to those of doctors, but can do so at far less expense, they often make up most of the staff at free or low-cost community clinics. They also help keep costs down at hospitals, hospices, nursing homes, college clinics, Veterans Administration facilities, and public health departments.

A number of nurse practitioners focus on women's and children's needs, which is a boon for the community clinics. These clinics help poor women get the care they need, especially all-important prenatal care, for either free or on a sliding scale. Nurse practitioners can act to help such women receive other aid, such as access to the Women, Infants and Children (WIC) program to improve both their nutrition and that of their offspring. Because nurse practitioners focus on education and wellness and can take more time with their patients, a trusting relationship can be established. Populations who may find the standard medical environment intimidating may feel comfortable enough to ask more questions and be more receptive to information about personal health and child-rearing. In this way, nurse practitioners can have a tremendous impact upon an entire community.

When working in obstetrics and gynecology (ob-gyn), a nurse practitioner provides contraceptive care and education; pelvic exams and Pap smears; treatment for vaginal infections; pregnancy testing; midwifery; STD screenings and follow-up exams; and screenings for more serious health conditions with referrals to physicians or specialists.

Nurse practitioners interested in travel and doing more for world health are very welcome in programs that work to bring affordable health care to places either financially or politically troubled. Regions where it is taboo for a woman to see a male doctor always need female nurse practitioners with a specialty in women's and children's care. A skilled nurse practitioner can do a great deal for the ob-gyn needs of this population. Even more, once they have developed a trusting relationship with their patients, they can engage in complex but necessary education. They can also do a great deal in the way of advocacy, particularly to governing bodies. It is understood that such work is very difficult and even dangerous to undertake, but it is desperately needed and the personal rewards will be tremendous.

Essential Gear

Good listening skills. A good nurse practitioner spends as much time listening as talking, mostly to patients but also to support staff and administration. In a community with a number of needs, a lot of attention must be paid to help patients effectively. Really communicating is key to being a genuine service provider.

For an aspiring nurse practitioner who hopes to work either abroad or at home on the community level, bilingual skills are not only useful, but almost necessary in some places. Translators are usually available, but if you want to build a strong bond with your patients and be useful to them in their community, you will do better if you can speak to them directly, rather than through a third party.

The majority of those who study to become nurse practitioners already have either an associate's or bachelor's degree in nursing, and many are presently working as registered nurses. In some instances, candidates can work toward their nurse practitioner degree while they are attaining their BSN, but most programs want not only the degree but also a record of working with patients with acute or chronic conditions. It is generally recommended, and in some places insisted upon, that a nurse practitioner have at least a master's degree. For those concerned about the costs of the program, schools often offer the opportunity to work as a staff nurse, and tuition reimbursements and grants are often available. You should expect to spend about three years working toward the certification, although if you decide to pursue a doctorate, it may take longer. You should also be aware that once you have your degree, you will have to pass an exam for your state license and in some instances, licensing may demand additional requirements. Also, you will probably want to apply for national certification once you have your license, and you may need to get yet more certification in your given specialty.

Once you have completed all this education, you are ready to enter a field that will allow you more direct and involved patient care. The opportunity to combine the warm, personal aspect of nursing with a higher level of medical care can be rewarding, and you can enjoy personal and professional satisfaction throughout your career.

You Are Here

Set yourself on the path to becoming a nurse practitioner.

Are you working as a nurse in a specialty that will carry over? Nurses who work in surgery or emergency care, for example, may need to transition to a field that involves direct patient care if they want to apply for a master's degree to become a nurse practitioner. You can consult an advisor at the school you would like to attend to see if you can begin the education process while also working in this different arena. Depending upon your level of experience, this may be allowed. For nurses who already work in direct patient care with specialties in health issues such as ob-gyn, pediatrics, adult wellness, geriatrics, or mental health, transition is much easier because they already have field experience to ground them in the educational process.

Are you committed to working intensely with patients, including those in difficult communities? While this can be necessary for almost everyone in the medical profession, so many nurse practitioners work in community health clinics that anyone starting the degree program should be aware that they will have even more contact and involvement than they have experienced as a nurse and will literally be far more hands-on. The best nurse practitioners welcome this aspect, but you do have to be aware that if you have been working in a well-funded hospital, a free clinic in a disadvantaged area will be a very different experience, as will the patients, and you have to be sure you are someone who will embrace this challenge.

Are you bilingual? As mentioned above, many on the patient roster at clinics will not have English as their first language. While translators are typically on hand to assist with patient communication, part of what makes being a nurse practitioner so appealing is the chance to work more directly with patients as a caregiver and educator. Predominately, Spanish is the needed language, and fluency in Spanish will help land you a job almost anywhere. The more language skills you have, the wider range of job opportunities you will enjoy.

Organizing Your Expedition

Get everything in order as you prepare to become a nurse practitioner.

Get hands-on experience working with patients. You probably already have this as a nurse, but if you have been working in a non-patient care capacity, you must return to direct patient care as you begin your degree work. You may find it more useful to do one or two rotations in a several areas that interest as you, both as a way of determining how you would like to specialize as a nurse practitioner and to be absolutely sure that you have both the desire and capacity to do this kind of work. Being a nurse practitioner is more medically involved than being a nurse, and the work as a caregiver is more strenuous and potentially exhausting. No matter how many credits you already have, gaining at least a master's degree to be a nurse practitioner takes about two years, and possibly longer, so you want to be certain you are excited about stepping up to this level of medical involvement before you begin.

Navigating the Terrain

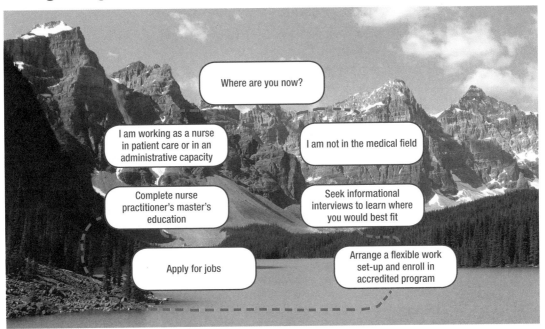

Take some language courses. While it is preferable if you are already bilingual, you can always make some time to master a few language skills. Someone who speaks fluent English and Spanish might also try to learn an Asian language, especially if they think they will be serving an area with a large immigrant population. If you are Vietnamese-American and speak the language, you will certainly be desired in a clinic serving other members of that community. If you think you would be interested in working in an African country, a solid grounding in French will help you in several of African nations. If you land a job as a medical worker in an area where English is not the predominant language, you should try to master at least some basic phrases in the primary language there. No one expects you to become fluent, but it does a great deal to break the ice if you show people the respect of trying to speak their language, and language skills will help you better understand patients and educate them.

Learn cultural practices in a given community. While being fluent in Spanish will cover you for a lot of work, it is also useful to know something about how a given community approaches to health care. If you

Notes from the Field
Jennifer Hoffman
Nurse practitioner, Maria de los Santos Center
(Delaware Valley Community Health)
Philadelphia, Pennsylvania

What were doing before you became a nurse practitioner?

My first college degree was in biology, and after graduating I worked for a year and a half as a medical assistant/receptionist until I figured out what career I wanted to pursue. During the latter half of this time period I also took prerequisite courses for the two nursing BSN-MSN programs that I was applying for. When I finished the undergraduate part of the program I had enrolled in, I worked as a nurse in a hospital and completed the graduate portion of my program part-time.

Why did you decide to pursue being a nurse practitioner?

I've always wanted a career in health care where I help people. I like the autonomy and independence that a nurse practitioner (NP) has in practicing, but also the increased preventative care, holistic and personable approach that I feel NP's are taught in school, in comparison to physicians. I like the flexibility that my specific degree gives me as a family nurse practitioner. I had baseline training in caring for adults, children, geriatrics, and ob-gyn, so I can practice in multiple areas of medicine, or change areas of practice when I feel it is time for something new. I actually have already functioned as both a pediatric and ob-gyn NP in the office I work in.

What was involved in terms of the education/training and securing your first job?

A newly graduated NP often requires more training on a new job than a physician because NP program clinical rotations are much shorter than a physician's three years of residency. It therefore took some time to find the specific job I was looking for—ob-gyn—because I found that often a practice this specialized is looking for an experienced NP who is able to jump in from day one and practice independently. The job I found last January took two months to find as well as two additional months to secure but is a perfect match for me. They [the community health center] are a partially publicly funded yet private health care organization functioning as a clinic for mostly uninsured and Medicaid patients. They were willing to train me for a few months and for the most part have been patient with questions.

What are the keys to success in this field?

A major key to success is the ability to work efficiently and to focus on important details during each patient encounter. Patients may bring up many details and problems, but with the time allotted with today's health care system, you must focus on what is important, and bring patients back if you need to. However, you also must be able to think critically about a patient complaint, and rule out all potential likely diagnoses. So you must be complete and focused at the same time, which remains a common challenge for many new health care providers.

You must be able to work effectively with many different people, including patients, peers, support staff, and administration. You have different relationships with these people, and will learn to master delegating, assisting, teaching, as well as learning. Do not assume any expectations, particularly of patients. You will encounter every type of patient, including those who do not care about their health. Also, you will learn not to judge patients, in order to gain their trust and maximize their ability to be compliant.

There is also a balance between a nurse practitioner trusting his or her personal knowledge and opinion and a nurse practitioner treating patients of which he or she is not experienced or even expected to care for. Know your limits and ask for help when you need it in order to safely care for your patients. You may need to refer your patients to another provider's care in your office in some situations. Talk with a supervising peer when training to establish guidelines and limitations. Otherwise, trust your judgment and experience because a nurse practitioner is a professional, respectable addition to any medical practice. You will learn mostly by experience on the job, and will also gain confidence when patients return to the office saying that your treatment helped them.

understand dietary traditions, lifestyle, parent-child relationships, etc., you will better be able to communicate to your patients. People who traditionally eat a high-sodium, high-fat diet and for whom exercise is a luxury run a number of health risks. You want to show that you understand and respect their traditions and obstacles, while also guiding them with practical, appropriate guidelines for improving their overall wellness.

Balance autonomy with effective teamwork and communication. Many nurse practitioners choose their field and enjoy it because it allows them a great deal of autonomy to deal with patients directly and in the manner they consider effective. You will also have colleagues, support staff, administration, and specialists to work with and the only way you and the clinic will be successful is if you are someone who can listen and work well with a variety of people who have radically different opinions and needs. You want to form strong relationships with physicians to whom you will refer patients, and you want to have a good understanding of how those physicians work with their patients, so that you will not send a patient with a certain temperament to a physician whose style will be antagonistic to that patient.

Essential Gear

Knowledge of government programs. You may often work with Medicaid, Medicare, the Veterans Administration, and state and even county-based programs. You should be well versed on all their various rules and procedures at any given time to be able to make your patients' and clinic's financial transactions as smooth as possible.

Landmarks

If you are in your twenties . . . If you think you want to become a nurse practitioner, you should first get your BSN and then work in direct patient care for a year or two before applying for the master's degree. If you are already nursing, take your time researching both a program and a specialty that you think you will be well suited for.

If you are in your thirties or forties . . . If you have job and family requirements that make the prospect of a few more years of education daunting, most programs have an option of part-time schooling. You will cut down on the time spent earning your license if you are in a nursing field that will translate directly to a nurse practitioner specialty and can continue to do this work as you study.

If you are in your fifties . . . If you working in a private office or hospital, you should be able to dovetail on-the-job training with your paid work and schooling. In rural areas where access to health care is limited, a nurse practitioner can even open a private office.

If you are over sixty . . . If you are a member of an immigrant community with which you would like to work, there should be a number of grants available to help you pay for schooling. A community that looks to medical professionals as respected elders will gravitate toward you very naturally and you may have far better success at such a clinic than someone half your age.

Further Resources

American Academy of Nurse Practitioners An invaluable site for anyone interested in learning about or becoming a nurse practitioner. It offers a wealth of detailed information on the profession and a number of useful links and publications. www.aanp.org
National Association of Nurse Practitioners in Women's Health For those who specialize in women's health, the association offers further education, news, forums, a job bank, and other member services. The NPWH is dedicated to the protection and promotion of individual women's rights to govern their health and well-being. http://www.npwh.org
State associations Because licenses are granted by states and requirements vary, most states have their own association of nurse practitioners. Find the one for your state to get more information on educational and work opportunities.

Physician Assistant

Physician Assistant

Career Compasses

Guide yourself to a career as a physician assistant.

 **Relevant Knowledge** of your specialty and the constant changes in the field (40%)

 **Caring** about your patients and the community (25%)

 **Communication Skills** to work effectively with patients, family members, and other caregivers and medical professionals (25%)

 **Organizational Skills** to maintain records and manage a busy office (10%)

Destination: Physician Assistant

 Sometimes confused with a medical assistant, whose work is more clerical combined with some routine clinical procedures, this fast-growing profession is in fact much closer to being a doctor. Physician assistants (PAs) perform about 80 percent of the tasks that doctors do. Physician assistants are supervised by physicians and surgeons, but they still work with a certain degree of autonomy. They conduct exams, make diagnoses, prescribe medication, and assist in surgery. Usually they are integral members of a health team, delegated by the doctor to perform given

tasks or provide services. They take histories, order and analyze tests, treat minor injuries, make notes on progress, provide counseling, and order or perform therapy. Depending upon the medical facility where the PA works, they may also take on managerial tasks such as ordering supplies and supervising technicians.

The comparatively new profession was developed in the 1960s when the shortage of doctors—particularly in underprivileged or remote areas—meant that many people's health needs were not being met and something had to be done quickly at a price that was manageable. Both nurse practitioners and physician assistants were brought into the field to combat the problem. A doctor who had been in the Navy developed the initial PA curriculum, based on the accelerated training military doctors receive during wartime.

Essential Gear

Technology skills. Telemedicine is a growing field, wherein technology is used to assist the consultations between physicians and physician assistants, as in rural areas where a physician might be on site only one or two days a week. Being comfortable and experienced with changing technology will make you a more desirable job candidate.

With the costs of maintaining health facilities high and constantly growing, physician assistants are increasingly being hired as a way of keeping costs down because they command a smaller fee than a fully qualified doctor. Free or low-cost clinics often find hiring a full-time doctor to be cost prohibitive so they turn to PAs. A PA might be the top medical professional at these clinics, with a doctor coming in one or two days per week. The PA discusses all relevant points with the supervising doctor and any other health professionals, depending upon necessity and state law. In instances where a patient is unable to get to the health care facility, such as in rural areas where such travel can be difficult, the PA—rather than the attending doctor—may make a house call and then discuss the case with the doctor.

When considering becoming a physician assistant, you should choose whether you want to go the medical or surgical route, much the same as if you were preparing to become a full physician. While the time spent attaining your degree and license to become a physician assistant is considerably shorter than becoming a full doctor, you still want to have your focus set. For medical work, you can concentrate on a number of specialties, including general internal medicine, pediatrics, family medicine, emergency medicine, orthopedics, and geriatrics. You can also do general and thoracic surgery (focusing on the chest cavity), which is separate from a surgery specialty. That involves providing pre- and postoperative care and working as a first or second assistant during a major operation.

Your schedule and daily activities vary depending upon the facility where you work. If you do surgeries, you are likely to have regular operations scheduled throughout a day and be on call as well. A clinic-based PA may keep standard hours from morning till evening, seeing patients and reporting to the doctor on staff, or making notes for a biweekly report. A hospital-based PA works shifts similar to that of doctors and nurses, including weekends, nights, and being on call.

The training necessary for qualification is much quicker than that for a doctor, which is part of what makes the profession appealing, especially to someone transitioning from another field who does not have the time to devote several years to a training program. The actual coursework lasts two to three years and most programs require that you have at least two years of college already and some experience in health care. When you have completed your accredited program, you also have to pass the Physician Assistant National Certifying Examination. You also must successfully complete 100 hours of further education every two years in order to retain your certification, and you have to take a recertification exam every six years as well. Additionally, each state has its own laws determining what a physician assistant may and may not do. You should be aware of these parameters before you look to perform a given specialty in a particular state.

The bulk of applicants to PA educational programs already have a bachelor's degree, and many work in the health care arena, predominantly as nurses or related health professions like paramedics. It is a reasonable transition because you already have a solid grounding in medical procedure and patient care, and within a few years you can be working with more autonomy and at a higher salary.

Upon a successful graduation and application for license, you are virtually guaranteed immediate employment because this is a fast-growing profession—especially if you are open to the idea of working in a rural area or an inner-city clinic where the need for affordable quality health care workers is strong. But hospitals, private doctor's offices, educational facilities, and even prisons are all looking to hire more physician assistants. You can even set up an office for yourself. Whether you will be teaching, providing valuable assistance in a medical or surgical capacity, or part of an important team in a clinic, you will be doing great work that you can be proud of.

You Are Here

Determine if you are ready to become a physician assistant.

Do you already have health care experience? Most of the physician assistant educational programs want you to have some basic health care experience as a prerequisite for application. Whether you work as a nurse, a physical therapist, occupational therapist, military medic, or home health aide, some direct patient care experience is looked for in prospective physician assistants. While you will get some training in school and on the job, schools want to see that you already understand and are successful at hands-on treatment. It is also important for you to be aware that this career path is what you want.

Are you self-motivated? Although you will not spend a lot of time in the classroom gaining your degree, if you want to remain in the profession, you will have to carry on with your education as you work. Depending upon where you are working, that may mean a lot of self-teaching and online coursework, as well as constant reading. To be a good physician assistant, you have to keep learning, and you have to be someone who is excited by the prospect of learning something new all the time.

Do you work well with others? While you will enjoy a certain amount of autonomy, wherever you are, you will be under the supervision of a physician. You have to be someone who enjoys being a member of a team and can communicate your thoughts and concerns but yields to a different opinion if that is how a decision is made. You will be respected and listened to, but being a physician assistant, even if you are self-employed, is all about being a team player, and you have to be someone who works well under those circumstances. Good communication is important both with the patient and the attending physician.

Navigating the Terrain

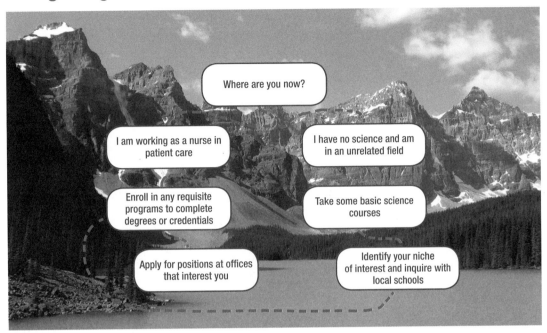

Where are you now?

I am working as a nurse in patient care

I have no science and am in an unrelated field

Enroll in any requisite programs to complete degrees or credentials

Take some basic science courses

Apply for positions at offices that interest you

Identify your niche of interest and inquire with local schools

Organizing Your Expedition

Be ready for whatever comes as you prepare to become a physician assistant.

Determine where you would like to specialize. Deciding whether you want to go into surgical or medical care is easy for some people, but most students take their time.

A variety of rotations can help you find your place, but the accelerated nature of the educational program means that you will do better if you have a sense of what you want at the outset. If you are already in nursing specializing in medical care and think that is where you want to stay, that is very useful, but you may ask the hospital where you work to put you on a surgical rotation before you make up your mind. You may find you have an interest and talent hitherto undiscovered. Likewise, someone doing surgical work may find that they are better with diagnoses and medical treatment. You will feel more confident and be a

Notes from the Field

Meggan Macias
Physician assistant, Child First Pediatrics
Centennial, Colorado

What were you doing before you became a physician assistant?

I originally thought I was going to do the straight liberal arts path, although I ended up majoring in psychology for my BA. I wasn't sure what I wanted—I either wanted to be a teacher or a social worker and knew psychology would be good for both. Then I took some of the standard science courses for the degree and discovered, to my surprise, that I was really good at it. I saw that if I got into medicine, I could combine all my interests. I could work kids and do counseling.

Why did you decide to become a physician assistant?

I didn't want to become an MD for a few reasons. First, I didn't want to have to be that much of a businessperson, which you really have to be as an MD these days. Also, and this is important, I wanted to have a family. I didn't even know the profession existed until I was in my junior year of college, but once I found out about it, I knew it was for me. It is much more conducive to a family life. After three years of postgraduate education, you can start seeing patients, and there is no problem with taking maternity leave. It was perfect.

What was involved in terms of education/training and getting your first job?

I had to make sure I had all my prerequisites and take the GRE. Before I started school, I worked in a pediatric medical office, which emphasized

stronger degree candidate if you know what you want going in and have the experience to back up that decision.

Take some language courses. As with nurse practitioners, physician assistants are most in demand in inner cities and areas with poorer immigrant populations. This means many of your patients will not have English as their first language. If you have the ability to speak in your patients' primary language, you will be more effective at your job. If you are already fluent in Spanish, this will open up far more job opportunities for you. Asian languages may also be useful.

to me how much I wanted to be in pediatrics. That's useful—it's good to know what you want to do. It's also good to see other specialties and know what you don't want to do. For the first year of school, it was all classroom work. The second year is half classroom, half clinic. The third year is all clinic. That's when most people determine where they'd like to go. We did 11 one-month rotations in that year. One of my last rotations was at a pediatric office that needed a PA, and they offered me the job. Of course, before I could begin seeing patients, I had to take the boards and get my license. But there was a lot to do and learn on the job while I was waiting: billing, scheduling, handling codes. Frankly, I could have done with more time learning some of those things before I got down to the real work.

What are the keys to success as a physician assistant?

You have to want to work hands-on with people. You have to have a lot of compassion. If you've spent the whole day seeing people with the same illness, by day's end it can wear on you, but you remember that you got into this profession to help people, and so you bring the same energy to the last patient of the day as you did the first. One of the most important things is that you must have a strong desire to always learn. Medicine is not static. You have to keep up with the journals, be flexible, and be excited about new innovations. You will always be learning throughout your career.

Get more clinical experience. You will do a number of rotations throughout your degree work (meaning you will rotate through different jobs), but you should push for even more diversity in your experience, rather than just fulfilling the requirements. If you are interested in ob-gyn, for example, look to do more with pediatrics and adult health as well. Ask for opportunities to work in occupational and mental health. You do not want to be a jack-of-all-trades, but you want to be well-rounded and have a good grounding in a variety of health issues. Besides, if you do end up working in a remote area, you may not have a large team and so the more you know about general aspects of health, the better a job you will do.

Make sure your bedside manner is excellent. Whether as the primary caregiver or essential member of a team, even if you are working in surgery, you should be someone who communicates well with patients and can offer good advice and genuine comfort. Additionally, since you may find yourself working with your supervisor off-site, you should be someone who can assess a condition and make a decision quickly. You have to trust your instincts and be clear-headed and quick-thinking.

Landmarks

If you are in your twenties . . . If you are already in medicine in some capacity, take your time determining where you would like to focus. If you do not have the option of trying out different areas in rotation, ask for informational interviews to help you decide. You should also take your time researching where you would like to work and what program you would like to attend.

Essential Gear

Interest in further education. Besides having to keep up with their education to maintain their licenses, physician assistants can also pursue postgraduate degrees in such fields as internal medicine, rural emergency care, emergency medicine, surgery, and pediatrics. Further education on this level will lead you to work with more responsibility and bigger paychecks.

If you are in your thirties or forties . . . If you have been working in nursing or something similar, now is a great time to look for a career change that will involve more responsibility and higher pay. If you do not want to relocate, ask your advisor about work opportunities in your area.

If you are in your fifties . . . If you have some medical or administrative experience, get yourself into a program to further your knowledge and your bona fides. Save time in the preparation process by ascertaining early in the process where you want to end up. For some positions and programs, you may be able to do coursework as you work in a entry-level job.

If you are over sixty . . . You should seek out training programs that put an emphasis on placing you in an earning position while you earn your credentials. You may have a rich network of professionals to reach out to for referrals and recommendations to get you started. You may have an advantage with private practices where most patients are elderly. Attentiveness and understanding are key skills for physician assistants; play to your strengths.

Further Resources

American Academy of Physician Assistants A membership organization devoted to the promotion of physician assistants as vital members of the health care profession who will help all Americans gain access to quality care. The AAPA offers a job board, licensing information, publications, news, and member benefits. http://www.aapa.org

Physician Assistant Forum An active forum with a number of boards for discussion and questions. http://www.physicianassistantforum.com

National Association of Physician Assistants A fairly new organization designed to promote the field and educate the public and health care world about the important work of physician assistants. The organization is actively seeking members dedicated to promoting the profession. http://www.nationalassociationpa.com

Chiropractor

Chiropractor

Career Compasses

Guide yourself to a career as a chiropractor.

Relevant Knowledge of anatomy, physiology, neurology, and all aspects of treating musculoskeletal disorders (40%)

Caring about the patient and the parameters of their complaint (25%)

Communication Skills to work effectively with patients, your network of related specialists, and to educate the public and medical community about the validity of science-based chiropractic medicine (25%)

Organizational Skills to run a business and maintain patient files (10%)

Destination: Chiropractor

Although the profession of chiropractor has existed for more than 100 years, it remains highly controversial. There are those who tout it as an excellent treatment for people suffering back pain or other musculoskeletal problems, usually in tandem with physical therapy. Some in the medical community, however, dismiss the career because it is "alternative medicine" that is often opposed to using biotechnological and biomedical interventions. Qualified chiropractors can find it frustrating when their profession is denigrated because of some practitioners who mix their work with questionable practices and do not belong to professional associations, such as the National Association for Chiropractic Medicine or the Canadian Academy of Manipulative Therapists. All the same, some of the chiropractors who mix holistic care with their treatment do their patients a lot of good.

Chiropractic medicine is meant to manipulate the spine when the joints are out of alignment. Similar to a physical therapist, a chiropractor assesses a patient's condition and performs noninvasive treatments involving manual manipulation or stretching of compromised muscles and joint therapy to relieve pain and regain mobility. A chiropractor also incorporates heat or ice packs, massage, and ultrasound, depending upon the nature of the injury. They may also teach the patient some exercises to do at home to quicken healing and maintain strength. Under most circumstances, a physical problem should see improvement after a few visits.

Essential Gear

Communication skills and empathy. Lower back pain is often debilitating, and many patients will be depressed. Part of your job will be to talk to them realistically about their condition and explain, using compassion and understanding, the full extent of the prognosis and what they might expect. Some patients will not be able to regain their full spinal health, but you can help them be positive about what they can achieve and bring them on board as a team member in their own treatment process.

Although it is controversial, a number of chiropractic schools also stress a holistic aspect to the healing process. While holistic methods can work very well, depending upon the ailment under question, some question if spinal manipulation should be partnered with acupuncture, hair analysis, or allergy testing. Western medical professionals may not know much about Eastern medicine and philosophies of health, but many of these practices can help heal and maintain good health. So a school of chiropractic health that incorporates holistic methods is not necessarily something to shy away from, particularly if you are already aware of and experienced with holistic healing. What you want to confirm before you get on board is that the school where you train is properly accredited and that its graduates are licensed professionals with good reputations.

The science-based aspect of chiropractic medicine includes taking X-rays and conducting orthopedic and neurological exams. A chiropractor may determine that a patient with poor balance, for example, may need to see an ear, nose, and throat specialist. The chiropractor may also watch the patient walk, analyze sitting and standing postures, and determine what therapies need to be used to maximize health. In addition to the stretches, massage, and ultrasound, chiropractors may also use water, light, and electric therapy. They may also use tape or braces to help support the spine during the healing process. A chiropractor usually discusses exercise and injury management with the patient and factors that can impede progress such as lifestyle and stress.

Many chiropractors have a private practice, which requires the ability to manage an office. Others are part of a group practice, which can make the maintenance of both office and patient base easier. Chiropractors can specialize in such fields as sports injuries, neurology, orthopedics, pediatrics, or diagnostic imaging.

Becoming a chiropractor requires earning a Doctor of Chiropractic (DC) degree and then obtaining a license. A prospective applicant should have at least two years or 90 semester hours of college completed already with a good grounding in science, including organic and inorganic chemistry, biology, and physics, as well as liberal arts such as social science and English. It is expected that a bachelor's degree will eventually be the minimum requirement to begin chiropractic coursework. As of 2008, only 21 colleges in America are accredited by the Council on Chiropractic Education. Some of these award bachelor's degrees in partnership with a liberal arts college, which means you can combine your studies and earn your DC a year earlier than you would have otherwise. The first two years of study entails a combination of classroom and lab work focusing on anatomy, physiology, public health, microbiology, pathology, and biochemistry. For the next two years of coursework, the student works on manipulation and spinal adjustment and gaining clinical experience under supervision, performing diagnoses, and therapies. Once coursework and clinical work is complete, students then take national board exams, and, depending on their location, they may have to take state board exams as well. Additionally, most states require a chiropractor fulfill a certain number of further education courses per year to retain their license. If you wish, you can also gain a post-doctorate in a specialty such as orthopedics, neurology, sports medicine, nutrition, rehabilitation, radiology, industrial consulting, family practice, and pediatrics.

Chiropractors can only practice in a state where they are licensed, and some states have different requirements, so you should do your research carefully if you are planning to move. Increasingly, states are requiring that aspiring chiropractors complete a bachelor's degree before they go on to earn their DC, and that DC must be earned at an accredited chiropractic college. Different states require a different amount of hours spent in clinical work prior to granting the license, and may have their own state exam in addition to the national board exam.

The increased demand for alternative, noninvasive health care treatments means that the employment prospects for chiropractors are growing steadily. More than half of chiropractors are self-employed or in a group practice. It is a field of medicine that many people still do not fully understand, both in the public and in the medical environment as well, so becoming a chiropractor means you will not only have the challenge of helping people to improve their spinal health, you will also be working to promote the profession, so that more people can come to you rather than pursue a more invasive, and expensive, surgical option.

You Are Here

Determine if you have the spine for chiropractic medicine.

Are you an excellent observer? Part of being a good chiropractor is being able to detect small abnormalities in someone's physique. When people come in to see you, they will be complaining of back pain, but you need to be able to discern from their posture and way of standing, sitting, and walking what other problems they may have and what may be exacerbating or creating their current problem. Is one shoulder slightly higher than the other? When they walk, does one foot jut at an angle? When they sit, does their neck jut out? You should ask if they work at a computer all day and ask them to demonstrate their usual work posture. The more you can ascertain about people's complaints without the use of invasive X-rays or other expensive tests, the better a chiropractor you will be.

Do you have superb manual dexterity and are you in good condition? You do not need to be particularly strong to be a good chiropractor, but you do need to be able to physically guide and work people's

Navigating the Terrain

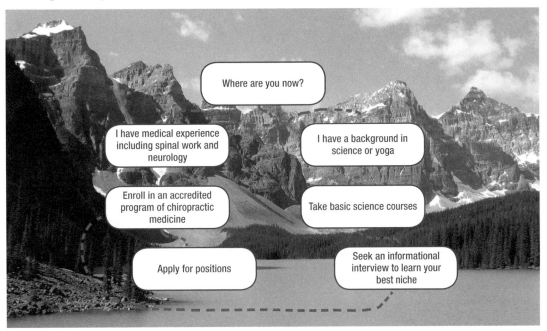

Where are you now?

I have medical experience including spinal work and neurology

I have a background in science or yoga

Enroll in an accredited program of chiropractic medicine

Take basic science courses

Apply for positions

Seek an informational interview to learn your best niche

bodies into proper position. Sometimes this involves bending over them as they are lying on their sides and twisting them to release air pockets, or manipulating their joints to help them perform stretches or other exercises. Or you may perform targeted massages. You use equipment to help you, but you have to be able to use your hands to do your best work. Furthermore, you have to not only have good dexterity but a sensitive touch so that you can locate the exact trouble spot and work it without aggravating it or anything around it.

Can you work independently and handle responsibility? Because many chiropractors work out of their own offices, you have to be someone who can manage a business as well as do your quality chiropractic work. Furthermore, while you probably will have a network of colleagues with whom you can consult on certain cases, they will not be available to you while you are dealing with the patient, so you have to be able to make the choice to treat someone on their initial visit or refer them to an osteopath (a doctor specializing in the musculoskeletal system) or

Notes from the Field

Robert A. Hayden, DC, Ph. D.
Iris City Chiropractic Center, PC
Griffin, Georgia

What were you doing before you got into chiropractic medicine?

I was a professional nurse for 20 years. I worked as a clinical specialist in cardiovascular health and it was a lot of fun—every day was different. But when a new bill was pushed through that affected nursing agencies, which would create excess regulations and have the effect of pushing down nursing salaries, the bloom starting coming off the rose, even though I still loved the blood and the gore and the drama.

Why did you decide to pursue chiropractic medicine?

My philosophy of health care was that I was there for the patient and accountable to them. But in a hospital, you're also accountable to a bean counter in the basement. I wanted balance. You need the bean counters, but I wanted my emphasis to be on the patient and saw I could get that through private practice. I wasn't sure which way to go until I was at a gathering and a man came in limping. After the meeting, a chiropractor there worked on the man for a little bit. With just a few spinal manipulations, he took the man's pain away. I had to know more about that! Also, I loved neurology and wanted to work more in that area.

What was involved in terms of education and training?

First, I did a lot of research and then went and knocked on doctors' doors, asking them what they did and how they did it. Then, I had to convince my wife I needed another doctorate. Once she was on board, I applied to the Life University School of Chiropractic in Marietta, Georgia. It is a four-year program, and you have to have two-and-a-half-to-three years of prerequisites, which I already had. Also, having been in the health profession that long, I already knew how to relate to patients and could deal with multidisciplinary issues, which helped a lot. Most programs want someone to have a college degree before they begin chiropractic study because they want students who are more mature and have more discipline. They're more efficient learners. You do your residency alongside your class work, making it a shorter program than med school. But really, it is once you get your license and start practicing that you start to seriously learn. You mold your practice based on your interests.

What are important qualities of a good chiropractor?

You have to be a people person. This is a hands-on field and you spend a lot of time talking to patients and working with them. Chiropractic medicine is about going after causes, not symptoms. You want to treat the whole person. You have to be a good observer and communicator. People don't always know how to explain their pain, and sometimes their nonverbal behavior can tell you more about what is going on than anything they say. You have to be an excellent diagnostician. A lot of the focus during your education is on diagnoses, and chiropractors are doing so well with them, medical schools are starting to pay attention to our system, because it is usually more effective. You have to have a lot of sympathy and empathy. Patients will often have more than just physical pain. Some will have severe disc injuries and are frightened that they won't be able to work and thus cannot feed their families. Some need counseling, because sometimes their pain is due to tension in their lives. Our idea is to try and get to the bottom of the cause. You also have to be adaptable and, unfortunately, a good businessperson. HMOs are difficult to work with and often don't remunerate in full. But our patient satisfaction is very high. My feeling is that it is all about the patient and I don't turn anyone away—so I sleep well at night. I know I have something wonderful to offer, and I get to see good results every day. I get to see people walking when they couldn't. A 23-year-old came in having suffered headaches since she was 16. During 10 days of working on her neck, she only had to take one painkiller. If it's true what they say and you get out of something what you put into it, we are very rich.

neurologist, depending on the nature of his or her complaint. You also need to remember that a lot of conditions may be beyond your scope, and you should be upfront with the patient about that.

Organizing Your Expedition

Get yourself ready to become a licensed chiropractor.

Find the school that will work for you. With so few properly accredited schools in the nation, you may have your work cut out for you finding one that is convenient. It is very important that you not be swayed by schools that claim to be fully accredited. For the most part, a school that focuses less on science-based chiropractic medicine and a more holistic overview is not going to teach you to be the sort of chiropractor who will actually improve people's spinal health. If you have an interest in holistic medicine, you should by all means seek training in that rapidly growing field, and if you want to practice it in addition to your chiropractic work, that will do a lot to expand your patient base. But your focus should be on becoming a properly licensed chiropractor, and for that, you must consult the Council on Chiropractic Education (CCE) for the appropriate schools.

Be financially prepared. A quality chiropractic education can be expensive, often more than $100,000. Unlike other medical school programs that are also costly, it is not a given that you will get a job that will pay well enough to help you start paying back those loans in a timely and comfortable manner. Furthermore, because chiropractic medicine still falls under the rubric of alternative care, you are less likely to qualify for grants or other reimbursements, as are available with degrees for becoming a nurse practitioner, for example. The job outlook is overall positive because more of the public and medical community is becoming interested in the possibilities of chiropractic medicine. There is also the reality of more people suffering from back problems due to the poor posture while sitting at desks. But many chiropractors find that they have to market their practice when they begin working. The best way to begin a practice, whether working as an individual or part of a group, is to build a patient base slowly, via good availability and good word of mouth. You can also be part of a network of physical therapists, personal trainers, practitioners of sports medicine, neurologists, and other such specialists so as to be on a doctor referral list. Many chiropractors enjoy financially successful careers, but be aware of the investment you have to make.

Maintain a realistic outlook. While the education you receive both at school and as you continue to practice should be science-based, you may encounter other possibilities of chiropractic medicine involving holistic medicine. Plus, as you practice, you may develop your own ideas about treatment—just be sure to maintain a scientific basis for your results, observing, recording, and reporting them. After all, chiropractic medicine is still comparatively new and, as with much about the workings of the human body and healing, much is unknown. Try to keep within reasonable boundaries. Some chiropractors swear that they can cure migraines, sciatica, and asthma. Indeed, they may have seen patients whose conditions improved after a round of chiropractic visits, but as with so much in medicine, when it sounds too good to be true, it probably is. Remember, your job is to put a skeletal system that is out of alignment back into place, and this must always be at the forefront of your practice.

Essential Gear

Membership in the National Association for Chiropractic Medicine. Next to your diploma from an accredited school, you should have proof of your membership in this professional organization. There will be some patients who come to you with skepticism, having heard stories of inept, uncredentialed chiropractors. You want to promote your profession positively and put a patient at their ease, as well as claim your place in the medical community with pride. This membership will help you do both.

Landmarks

If you are in your twenties . . . If you do not have family commitments, now is the time to look for a school that best suits your interests and desires, rather than having to factor in location as a consideration. You are also in a better position to take out a large loan, rather than have to search for a program that will allow you to do paid work while you study.

If you are in your thirties or forties . . . Location and a part-time program may be something you need to consider. If your chosen school does not offer a part-time program, talk to the advisor about the possibilities of lightening your course load so that you can work. If you are a qualified applicant, your school will likely be happy to try and accommodate your needs.

If you are in your fifties . . . If you have a background in nursing, physiology, or something similar, you may be able to do an accelerated program of study. You may also be able to combine staff work at a hospital with clinical hours, depending upon the program.

If you are over sixty . . . Again, a related background and recent education in some of the requirements should allow you to do an accelerated program. You will probably want to look for work within a group, rather than open your own office.

Further Resources

Council on Chiropractic Education This is the federally recognized agency for the accreditation of chiropractic schools. The CCE is committed to the quality of chiropractic education and is continually developing its criteria and assessing programs. The site gives you all necessary information on educational programs as well as access to useful publications, links, and the ability to contact them for further questions. http://www.cce-usa.org

American Chiropractic Association A membership organization that does public relations and funds research into chiropractic issues. It offers a variety of resources including a job board. http://www.amerchiro.org

State chiropractic associations Most states will have their own professional associations with pertinent publications, job boards, access to a discussion forum, information on insurance and liabilities, and other useful information.

Complementary/Alternative Medicine Specialist----

Complementary/Alternative Medicine Specialist

Career Compasses

Guide yourself to a career in complementary/alternative medicine.

Relevant Knowledge of your specialty and its parameters (25%)

Caring about your patients (40%)

Communication Skills to overcome patient skepticism and explain complex home therapies (25%)

Organizational Skills to run an office if you go into private practice (10%)

Destination: Complementary/Alternative Medicine Specialist

Also called "natural medicine," or abbreviated as CAM, this style of healing has long been used to good effect around the world since the beginning of civilization. After all, everything in medicine originally derived from nature in some fashion. In both the Eastern and Western worlds, herbs, exercises, and food have been used to heal illness and promote overall wellness. Over the last two centuries in particular,

Western medicine's proved efficacy has caused it to shun natural and alternative methods of healing, and in some cases, with good reason. However, over the past few decades, natural medicine has made inroads into Western thought and even some practice. While a lot of Western practitioners are skeptical of a natural approach to wellness, they acknowledge that it can often produce results more cheaply and less invasively than Western pharmaceuticals and procedures.

There are numerous forms of natural healing, all with long histories and complex methodologies. A few of them include: acupuncture, ayurveda (an ancient Hindu system of health care), colonics, herbalism, homeopathy, hydrotherapy, naturopathy, and traditional Chinese medicine (TCM). Forms of exercise such as tai chi and yoga are also incorporated into natural healing and wellness. Most of these forms of medicine embrace the philosophy that illness cannot be treated in isolation. That is, rather than just take a prescription antihistamine for hay fever, a practitioner of natural medicine examines issues involving the whole body to get at the root of the problem and then prescribe a formula of therapies and possibly herbs to overcome, rather than just manage, the problem. Pharmaceuticals eventually lose their potency, and you have to get a new prescription, whereas the thinking with natural medicine is that you use better wellness techniques and herbs to be healthier overall.

Obviously, Western science-based medicine is invaluable. Thanks to its advances, combined with improvements in infrastructure and public amenities, much of society is free of diseases that were once a regular part of life. Furthermore, serious illnesses like some cancers can now be cured; HIV/AIDS and other STDs that were once a death sentence are at least manageable; and illnesses like diabetes and asthma need to have almost no effect upon the person who lives with them. A good practitioner of natural medicine understands the value of Western medicine and does not underestimate its importance. Rather, he or she understands that natural methods can be good alternatives for some complaints and can work with Western medicine to improve health, much in the same way as allopaths should not dismiss natural healing but take note of how it can treat ailments without relying on chemicals or invasive techniques.

Even within Western medicine, it is understood that aspects of natural healing can promote wellness. Changes in diet and exercise have done a great deal to improve people's health in the last century as awareness and availability have given rise to modern prescriptions for daily fresh fruits and vegetables, as well as water, whole grains, and more plant-based proteins. Diet is at the base of much of natural healing. Some foods are proven to allay disease and even heal some illnesses. Whatever sort of natural medicine you end up practicing, some attention to diet will be paid.

As mentioned, many paths can be taken in the pursuit of holistic care. But it is generally agreed that there are five categories of natural medicine. They are: whole medical systems, mind-body medicine, biologically based practices, manipulative and body-based practices, and energy medicine. Very few of them are practiced without some overlap from another category.

Briefly, whole medical systems encompass practices like TCM and ayurveda. They consider the whole body when assessing a particular problem, and use aspects of the other categories in their treatments.

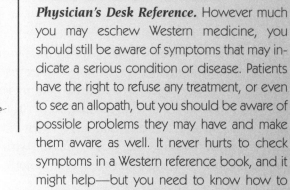

Essential Gear

Physician's Desk Reference. However much you may eschew Western medicine, you should still be aware of symptoms that may indicate a serious condition or disease. Patients have the right to refuse any treatment, or even to see an allopath, but you should be aware of possible problems they may have and make them aware as well. It never hurts to check symptoms in a Western reference book, and it might help—but you need to know how to use it!

Mind-body medicine is focused on the connections between the mind, body, and spirit—as exemplified in yoga or tai chi, which encourage calm and a healthy connection with body and thought. Massage and the Alexander technique can also fall into this category. Biologically based practices focus on the use of herbs and foods to heal and promote wellness. Manipulative and body-based practices believe that manipulation of the body can heal a variety of ills. This comprises chiropractic and osteopathic medicines. Some in the medical community consider energy medicine to be the most dubious form of complementary medicine. It suggests that healing can be accomplished using electromagnetic fields.

Anyone interested in pursuing a career in complementary or alternative medicine—CAM—can be encouraged by its growing popularity. People are turning to CAM in droves, whether they are frustrated by the lack of progress or satisfaction in Western medicine or just want to try something different. From drinking teas to support immunity or reduce headaches to using *neti* pots to relieve sinus infections to using acupuncture for pain, CAM is becoming a part of more people's lives. Even more encouraging, some Western hospitals and HMOs are incorporating alternative treatments into their health systems. Physicians are seeing the proof that some natural methods can really help people, and if they can be delivered more cheaply and less invasively, many doctors appreciate and support that. Some allergists are starting to recommend the use of a *neti* pot to their patients, and not just because they were a big hit on *Oprah*. The *neti* pot, a staple in ayurveda, is used to clean out the nasal passages with warm, salty water. Once people get over the "ick" factor, they find that it is an effective way of keeping nasal passages open longer, without chemicals, and they do not go back. As such natural methods gain wide acceptance, people may turn away from a reliance on pharmaceuticals and toward a more organic, low-impact approach to personal health.

The comparative newness of CAM means that very few schools are accredited for teaching practitioners. This number is expected to grow, but for now, it means that those who are interested in pursuing this work have to do a lot of research to find not only what path they wish to pursue but where they will get the best education. The only way CAM will continue to gain acceptance with both the Western medical community and the population at large is if quality practitioners apply it with good sense and skill. There will always be skeptics, but the more people see that at least some aspects of holistic healing actually have an effect, the more successful a career you will enjoy.

You Are Here

Find your path to a career in complementary/alternative medicine.

Have you used CAM personally? Virtually everyone who treats people with natural medicine has been treated with it, and this is often how they gain an interest in the profession. It helps to come to it from a personal standpoint because it gives you more confidence and understanding. Having found that it is effective for some ailments will generate continued research on your part. While some aspects are practiced much the same as they were hundreds of years ago or more, CAM specialists adapt and develop techniques to complement methodologies in Western practice and treat new ailments.

Do you have a basic grounding in physiology? Some health practitioners like to mix Western and natural treatment methods, whereas others eschew Western medicine completely. Which way you go is your choice. A quality educational program demands that you take science courses such as biology, anatomy, and physiology. The more you know already when you go in to a program, the more effective a practitioner you will be. A strong, clear-cut understanding of how the body works is absolutely essential. In particular, you want to be able to discern when a complaint might be more serious than is initially evidenced so that you can make the necessary recommendations.

Are you an excellent communicator and teacher? Many aspects of CAM involve long one-to-one discussions with patients. You may have to conduct procedures that patients will not have experienced before, such as analyzing their tongue. Some untraditional methods can arouse skepticism. You have to be able to explain why you are doing what you are doing and what it is telling you about their condition. You have to be prepared to explain your philosophy of health and treatment so that they will understand and follow through with your recommendations. You cannot assume that just because they have chosen to see you, it means they are ready to try everything you suggest. If you can clearly explain the procedures and what the patient might expect, they are much more likely to support their own care.

Organizing Your Expedition

Prepare yourself for the complex world of complementary/alternative medicine.

Do your research thoroughly. You have a lot of decisions to make. First and foremost, you need to select your field of medicine. You may already be inclined toward one, but you should take some time looking into and understanding the methodologies of some others before you decide on

Navigating the Terrain

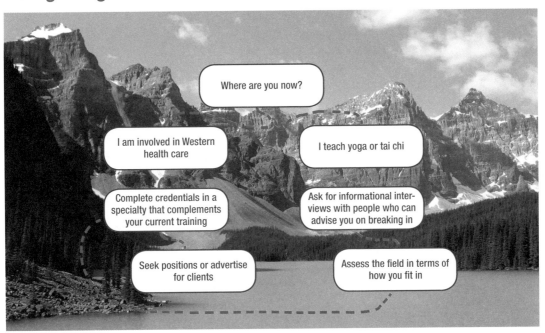

Where are you now?

I am involved in Western health care

I teach yoga or tai chi

Complete credentials in a specialty that complements your current training

Ask for informational interviews with people who can advise you on breaking in

Seek positions or advertise for clients

Assess the field in terms of how you fit in

your path. It may be that, while you thought you were an ideal herbalist, you should instead pursue acupuncture. Once you know for sure what you want to do, the much-harder step is obtaining strong training in the field. You can start by consulting the Council on Naturopathic Medical Education. This is the board that accredits programs that teach naturopathic medicine. Thus far, there are very few programs, but this number is expected to grow. You can also find accredited schools for homeopathy and aromatherapy, both of which are also expected to grow. For acupuncture, consult the Accreditation Commission for Acupuncture and Oriental Medicine. By far, this is where you will find the most programs, although you should note that the bulk of them are on the West Coast. For other specialties, contact the appropriate licensing board for information on educational and training programs.

Understand your limitations. Some say that natural medicine can cure cancer, HIV/AIDS, multiple sclerosis, and any number of fatal or otherwise serious diseases. Perhaps some symptoms respond to a natural

Notes from the Field

Karen Ann Lavallee-Tente
Licensed massage therapist
Easthampton, Massachusetts

What were you doing before you decided to pursue massage therapy?

I had received my BFA from the University of Connecticut. My major was photography, and my unofficial minor was painting. I was on the four-and-a half year plan! I then got a job at the *Hartford Courant* newspaper while still in college. I worked as a part-time photo lab technician/imaging technician. I was there for 16 years until I was laid off in 2005.

Why did you decide to pursue massage therapy?

I decided to try massage school because a bunch of people suggested it as something I might be good at and that I seemed interested in. One of my coworkers at the newspaper (I was still working there at the time) had suffered from shoulder and neck tension, and I gave them some uneducated bodywork. They said I had a natural ability. And then a friend of a friend talked up the school (The Connecticut Center for Massage Therapy), so I had to check it out. It was accredited and would allow me to maintain flexible hours with the *Courant.* I decided that doing an 18-month program would be manageable, and a part-time job as a massage therapist would be a nice complement to my *Courant* job. I also liked the idea of being able to make my own hours and, more importantly, work in a field where people were happy. Even if I couldn't do as much for a client as I might like, I knew that they wouldn't leave the office in any more pain, and most of them could be helped. That was very different from the corporate environment that prevailed at the paper. I loved my job at the paper, but there were always unhappy people and lots of

treatment, or some strains show improvement, but touting natural methods of treating such illnesses is a surer path to discrediting both you and the profession, rather than increasing your patient base. During your training, you may hear stories of someone coming back from the brink of death via herbs, and the stories may even be true, but you will do better to take them with a grain of salt and maintain your focus on more proven pressure in the office, especially toward the end when there was fear of job loss and low morale.

What was involved in terms of making the transition?

After I finished my program work and training, I was able to get a part-time job as a massage therapist and did that, along with my newspaper job, for a few years; although my goal was to get to a place where I was only doing massage therapy. Then I was laid off, which obviously forced the issue. I also got married and moved to Massachusetts, which made for some big changes. I'd been licensed in Connecticut of course, but then had to get a new license in Massachusetts. In getting more serious about doing the therapy work full time, I also got a national certification.

What are some keys to success/qualities that make a good massage therapist?

I work from the heart. Although of course I have to think in terms of business, I'm not in this to try to make money from people. In fact, I offer a lot of discounts and have a sliding scale. I want them to get what they need from a session, whether it is pain- or stress-relief or just relaxation. I am there to "hold the container" for that person and just give them my best. Every massage therapist has their own style and method. It is also important to maintain your national certification, which means continuing education. This is not only essential, it is fun! I love learning new techniques, or even just tweaking my old ones. And of course, the more abilities you have, the more clients you can draw. I have just been certified for prenatal massage and am currently working on my log hours to get registered as a Jin Shin Do (a type of acupressure) practitioner.

abilities. That is not to say you should be completely skeptical, but this is where a dose of cynicism can be healthy.

Build a network of healthcare professionals. A certain contingent of patients will come to you before seeing an allopath, whether because they do not trust Western doctors, do not have one, or do not think their condition warrants such treatment. While you should respect their concerns, if you discern that their condition is more serious than they think, you are obliged to inform them as much and at least suggest that they see an allopath. If they do not have a physician, or if their insurance plan offers some flexibility, you should have a network of professionals you trust and like to whom you can refer such patients. Likewise, of course, the members of the network should refer interested patients to you!

Maintain your education. As with many Western fields of medicine, natural fields are continually evolving. If you are not required to take regular coursework for maintaining your license, you should do your own research and attend regular meetings of peers so as to keep learning. Even an ancient tradition will have new developments.

Essential Gear

Knowledge of contraindications. Many patients who come to you may be taking some form of prescription or OTC medication. If you are an herbalist, you know what you cannot give someone with specific allergies, but you should also be able to quickly consult a proper guide to determine contraindications with chemical-based medications. Your patients sign waivers understanding that what you give them may not work, but you must be sure that you will not worsen their condition. Patients, too, need to know that herbs can trigger allergies so that they tell you their susceptibilities.

Landmarks

If you are in your twenties . . . Take your time researching the field you would like to work in. You might investigate the possibility of an internship to really get a sense of what the work entails. Ask for informational interviews as well, and consider taking additional science courses to have a fuller understanding of the body.

If you are in your thirties or forties . . . Consider how whatever you are doing now might transition well to complementary medicine. If you are involved with diet and nutrition in some way, there are a number of good options that mesh with that specialty. If you are in health care and experienced with physiology, you might consider acupuncture.

If you are in your fifties . . . Look for a program that might allow you to do on-the-job training or other paid work while you train. Fields like holistic nutrition are very welcoming of nurses and other health professionals who may want to turn their empathy skills and knowledge toward a more natural-based approach.

If you are over sixty . . . Look for a program that might pair you with a professional for hands-on training and teamwork. You may want to get into practice more quickly, and a specialty such as aromatherapy requires a shorter training period than homeopathy or acupuncture.

Further Resources

National Center for Complementary and Alternative Medicine The governmental agency for scientific research on CAM, it provides a wealth of information on various fields of CAM, training programs, research grants, and clinical trials. http://nccam.nih.gov

American Association of Acupuncture and Oriental Medicine Provides information for members, students, and consumers. It holds an annual conference and you can consult publications and press clippings. http://www.aaaomonline.org

Homeopathic Medical Association Based in the United Kingdom, it still provides useful information about current scientific research, education, and literature. http://www.the-hma.org

Osteopath

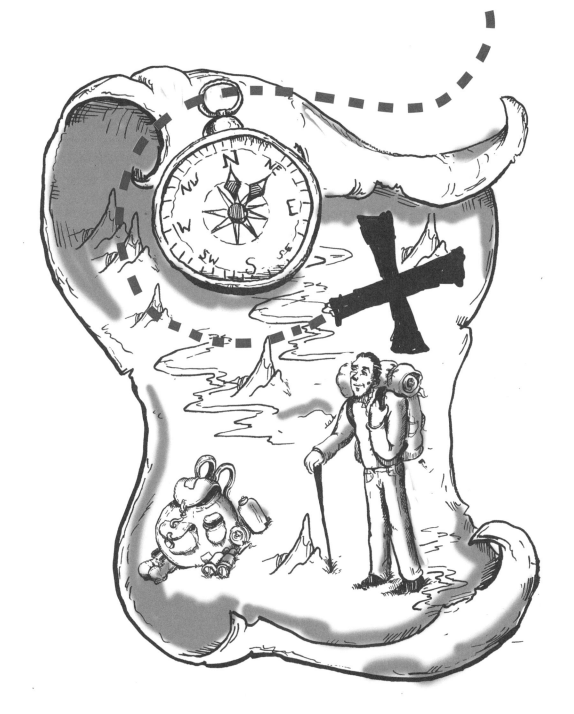

Osteopath

Career Compasses

Guide yourself to a career as an osteopath.

Relevant Knowledge of your specialty and the intricacies of the body (40%)

Caring about your patient's physical and emotional state (25%)

Communication Skills so that your patient understands the treatment and is fully committed to the process (25%)

Organizational Skills to maintain detailed patient records (10%)

Destination: Osteopath

Although mostly science-based, osteopathy is also considered a branch of holistic medicine. Similar to chiropractic medicine, it focuses on the musculoskeletal system and a system of healing that involves physical manipulation. However, doctors of osteopathy (DO) can also perform surgery and prescribe medication. Likewise, DOs must complete four years of medical school following a four-year bachelor's degree program. Then they undertake 300 to 500 hours of further hands-on training in manual medicine. They receive their license at the state level and, if they want to specialize in an area such as surgery or obstetrics, they must become board-certified, which requires a residency of anywhere from two to six years in the specialty and then passing a board exam. They are also required to take continuing education courses in order to remain certified. Some in the medical field look dubiously on osteopathy, and certainly some schools and osteopaths use some controversial methods. However, most accredited schools and properly licensed osteopaths are producing excellent results treating illness and injury with careful manipulations.

The idea of osteopathy is that the correct manipulations of a body will "free" it so that the body's own natural healing abilities will work without disruption. An osteopath must have a highly attuned sense of touch to feel the traumas in the body and work them out. In principle, the correct amount of force, gently applied, puts the body on track to heal itself. Tissues move freely and bones and joints that are compromised, injured, or compressed are set right. Additionally, an osteopath takes the mental state of the patient into consideration, noting that stress or depression has a physical impact upon the body and the immune system's functions. While this description can make some allopaths skeptical of osteopathy, the medical community as a whole is increasingly welcoming of osteopathic medicine, seeing that osteopathic manual medicine (OMM) can be of great use. Stress has been shown to harm the immune system and can affect the posture and other bodily aspects, and the manipulations used to relieve that stress can work effectively without invasive procedure or medication. Furthermore, a DO uses similar methods of diagnoses and some treatments as conventional medicine.

Essential Gear

Good teaching skills. No, you will not be approaching your patients as a teacher, but you should be thinking as one, at least in part. Since osteopathy is about helping the body to work at its top function and heal itself, the patients need to be enthusiastic about treatment. If they have doubts, that negativity can stand in the way of complete recovery. Your job is to help them thoroughly understand the treatment process and get them excited so that they will work with you to get well.

Although most people only see an osteopath when they are ill or injured, the science of osteopathy is equally devoted to preventive medicine. Maintaining a correct posture and system of movement will keep the immune system functioning normally. This school of thought was at the backbone of osteopathy as developed by Dr. Andrew Taylor Still during the Civil War, who observed that medical practices at that time could do as much to harm the patient as good. Dr. Still was interested in the power of the immune system and saw the musculoskeletal system as the core of general health, because the muscles, nerves, bones, and organs are all interrelated. In this sense, osteopathy is similar to holistic medicine and acupuncture in particular, which recognizes that nerves in the feet, for example, can be related to such organs as the liver and kidneys. Even the most skeptical allopaths recognize that some illnesses cannot be fully treated in isolation and that there is great value in both encouraging the body to assist in its own recuperation and assessing the body as a whole when diagnosing a complaint.

Rather than use instruments like stethoscopes, osteopaths use their hands to diagnose and treat their patients. DOs feel the back, joints, tendons, ligaments, and muscles, assessing them both for pain and possible motion restrictions that indicate deeper injury or impaired function. While the focus may be on the back—since the spine has so many nerves and is the body's core—the process of diagnosis and treatment is more specific than chiropractic medicine. Osteopathy focuses more on the injury and how it can create other symptoms.

While 20 accredited schools of osteopathy are in the United States, and a properly licensed DO can practice in fully accredited hospitals and medical centers, there is a branch of osteopathy that many in the medical community, including osteopaths, regard with concern. This is cranial therapy, also called *craniosacral therapy* or tag *cranial osteopathy*, which claims that the skull's bones can be manipulated to relieve pain. Some parents unable to relieve their infant's colic or ear infections have turned to cranial therapy and reported good results, as have other sufferers of chronic pain. However, many board-certified osteopaths consider cranial therapy to be an unsupported practice, and it remains controversial and not a typical aspect of the science of osteopathy.

Osteopathic schools focus on primary care, with more than half of licensed osteopaths working in pediatrics, ob-gyn, and internal medicine. In addition to hospitals, osteopaths practice in clinics and private offices. Many insurance providers cover the cost of a visit to an osteopath, making it increasingly easier for osteopaths to secure jobs or open their own offices.

While admission to osteopathic schools is competitive, and most students have a science or health background, osteopathy is also a common second career, so those who have not previously been involved in science or health should not shy away from pursuing the degree. Osteopathic schools assess candidates on the basis of personality, background, and approach to medicine as much as aptitude, experience, and test scores.

If you are interested in the practice of medicine while not following an exactly conventional route, and you are excited about the possibility of treating people using noninvasive techniques while encouraging the body to function at its best capacity, you should certainly explore the growing world of osteopathy.

You Are Here

Determine if you are on the right path for osteopathy.

Do you have a bachelor's degree in a scientific field or equivalent experience? To be accepted into the four-year educational program to become an osteopath, you must have a bachelor's degree in a health or life science field. While there are undoubtedly successful applicants with a BA, rather than a BS, they most likely have nearly perfect MCAT (Medical College Admission Test) scores and experience in the medical arena. As with the profession itself, a school assesses the candidate as a whole, so GPA and MCAT scores, as well as bachelor's degrees, are not be the sole focus in gaining admission. A clinical background and a demonstrable passion for helping patients can help you gain admittance. The bulk of students are recent graduates, but nearly a quarter of aspiring osteopaths have come to medicine as a second career.

Are you prepared to spend up to four years getting your education? For those who come to osteopathy from another area of health care, such as nursing, physical therapy, occupational therapy, or chiropractic medicine, a school may give credit for previous courses and experience, and this can reduce the time required to complete your training. For the most part, however, you must be prepared to dedicate up to four years for your schooling. Plus, depending on your specialty and previous experience, your residency can take at least another two years.

Navigating the Terrain

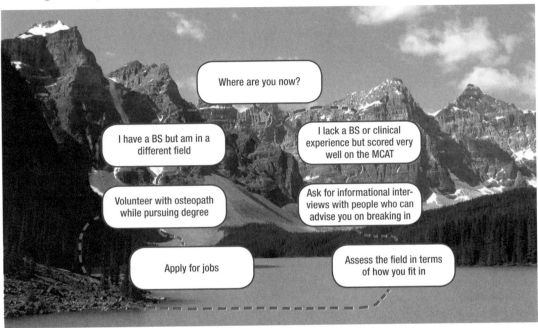

Where are you now?

I have a BS but am in a different field

I lack a BS or clinical experience but scored very well on the MCAT

Volunteer with osteopath while pursuing degree

Ask for informational interviews with people who can advise you on breaking in

Apply for jobs

Assess the field in terms of how you fit in

Are you sensitive and good with your hands? The training you will receive will help you if you are already someone who has a highly refined sense of touch. A good osteopath can discern the smallest misalignment in a muscle just by feel. If you have always had a strong tactile sensibility, and especially if you have applied that in an area of patient care, you may be uniquely qualified to enter the world of osteopathy.

Organizing Your Expedition

Prepare yourself for the hands-on world of osteopathy.

Shadow an osteopath. The specialized nature of osteopathy, with its combination of scientific and holistic methods and philosophies, is not for everyone, and the best way for you to know if you are suited for the field is to get some real experience first. "Shadowing" an osteopath at his or her job is a great way to see if the career is a good match. Plus, many of the osteopathic colleges want candidates who have a letter of

Stories from the Field

Miriam V. Mills
MD, FAAP (Fellow of the American Academy of Pediatrics)
Tulsa, Oklahoma

Dr. Miriam Mills, a pediatrician at the Young People's clinic in Tulsa, Oklahoma, directed one of the most important research projects on the effects of osteopathic manipulative treatment for children's ear infections, published in 2003 in the peer-reviewed journal *Archives of Pediatric and Adolescent Medicine.* Dr. Mills saw that incorporating some forms of osteopathy into her treatment resulted in fewer instances of colic, feeding problems, headaches, and ear infections, as well as fewer admittances to hospitals or referrals to specialists.

She had already been a medical doctor for a number of years when she developed an interest in osteopathic medicine in 1987, after having been injured in a car accident. Part of her treatment included osteopathic manipulation. The noninvasive and yet hugely effective techniques impressed her so much, she decided to enter training in the field and apply the practices of osteopathy in her own specialty of pediatrics.

Dr. Mills is delighted with the positive effects of osteopathic medicine on her patients. She combines the standard techniques of observation—seeking to identify obstacles that are keeping the body from performing at its top function—as well as the stretching, positioning, and unwinding that removes obstacles and resets the body when it is compromised. She also uses the slightly more controversial techniques of head and sacrum (triangular bone at the base of the spine) manipulation.

recommendation from an osteopath as part of their application. Even if the school to which you are applying does not require shadowing or a letter of recommendation (although most will), you should still take any opportunity to work with a DO, as this will help you with the interview process of application. Finally, it will demonstrate your commitment to the field. Schools or local business listings may provide leads.

Meet with a student ambassador. Too many medical students, even those who begin their study with great passion and excitement, burn

It is this that she has found can be a real boon for children with recurring ear infections, sinus infections, and colic. She has even observed it to be helpful in the treatment of asthma.

Dr. Mills differentiates her practice of cranial osteopathy from what is called "craniosacral therapy" and practiced by some chiropractors, massage therapists, and physical therapists. The methods she uses are based strictly on principles of osteopathy.

In a six-month long study, Dr. Mills examined children in four locations throughout the United States who were in either a control or treatment group. It was shown that those in the treatment group showed a marked decrease in the occurrence of ear infections, and required fewer antibiotics than those in the control group.

An osteopathic pediatric session lasts anywhere from 20 to 40 minutes, and three or four sessions per week for two weeks may be required before progress can be observed. Dr. Mills will see patients periodically over several months to note their development and determine if the treatment needs to be altered. This is especially necessary for children, whose bodies are constantly developing.

The demand for osteopathic treatment is on the rise, as more doctors and patients see results from this non-invasive form of medicine. Dr. Mills stresses the importance of adequate training at a proper school. She also notes that for those who want to work with children, some creativity is required. As any parent knows, it can be a tall order to ask a child to lie still for five minutes, let alone 20 or 40, so Dr. Mills distracts her young patients with toys while they are receiving treatment.

out quickly once they confront the arduous coursework and sometimes infuriating politics of medical school and the medical community. If you have little to no medical background, you should arrange to meet with one or more student ambassadors from an osteopathy program. Prepare your questions and concerns beforehand (although they will always be happy to meet with you again or answer questions via phone or e-mail). Student ambassadors want to talk up their program and get people excited about joining, but they also want you to understand all the parameters before you get in. If you have not been in a classroom setting in a while, you must be prepared for some extremely hard work, and ambassadors will give you the real details about what is required to successfully handle the training and education.

Be sure you see patients as people, not symptoms. Some medical professionals see patients as simply "frequent migraines" or "chronic cough," or "mild scoliosis," rather than a whole person who may be exhibiting a symptom or has a condition. In osteopathy, professionals are not only hands-on, they spend time getting to know their patients as a whole so they can understand their overall condition and assist them in achieving better health. In this career, you must be compassionate, communicative, and excited about regularly coming into contact with a wide range of people. These qualities will make you an excellent osteopath who can get the complete picture of a patient's health.

Essential Gear

An appreciation of rigor and the scientific method. The accredited osteopathic college you attend will teach you on a scientific basis, but as you read more literature and meet more osteopaths, even including students in your labs, you will see that the holistic aspect has a lot of shading. Some students swear they can feel someone's electric field pulsing, for example. You can believe such things if you like, but osteopathy is a holistic practice with a scientific grounding, so you must put certain methods in perspective and apply them with caution.

Investigate financing opportunities. Everyone knows medical school is not cheap. Fortunately, scholarships and loans are available for aspiring osteopaths, and you may even find part-time work during your training to help meet expenses. If you are concerned about taking on a heavy debt load, concentrate on finding scholarships and grants for which you may be eligible. Financially disadvantaged students may have their tuition costs waived.

Landmarks

If you are in your twenties . . . If you are fresh out of college with a BS, you should consider doing a year or so of clinical work either as a volunteer or assistant before looking for a DO to shadow and applying to an osteopathic college. While the bulk of students are recent college graduates, someone with a more diverse background will stand out.

If you are in your thirties or forties . . . If you have a non-scientific background, look for volunteer opportunities to familiarize yourself with clinical practices and procedures while you prepare to take the MCAT and other admissions tests. While shadowing a DO can take as little as a few days, ask if you can do it longer, or shadow more than one to immerse yourself in the work.

If you are in your fifties . . . If you are coming from a medical background such as pediatric nursing, you may be able to do the degree in three years, rather than four, although you probably will not be able to do it in less time than that. If you are at a hospital with an osteopathic department, ask if you can do a rotation there while you are applying for school.

If you are over sixty . . . You should probably be working in medicine already with a lot of clinical experience and in a related field like pediatrics or ob-gyn. A diverse background and further experience with something like massage can be very helpful when embarking on this career path.

Further Resources

American Association of Colleges of Osteopathic Medicine This should be your first port of call in looking for an osteopathic college. This group not only lists accredited programs, it gives you detailed information on the application process, financial aid, and the coursework. The group also offers publications, a job board, and a calendar of events. http://www.aacom.org

The Osteopathic Research Center The ORC focuses on collaborative research and the continuing developments in osteopathy. It is an excellent source for further education and resources. http://www.hsc.unt.edu/orc

American Osteopathic Association A membership organization to promote the philosophies and practices of osteopathy. Learn the association's viewpoints, but be aware that they do not represent the mainstream of current medical thinking. http://www.osteopathic.org

Pharmacist

Pharmacist

Career Compasses

Guide yourself to a career as a pharmacist.

Relevant Knowledge of drugs and drug therapies, including interactions and side effects (25%)

Mathematical Skills to calculate dosages and weights (25%)

Communication Skills to work effectively with patients and family members (25%)

Organizational Skills to maintain records, multitask, and sort medications (25%)

Destination: Pharmacist

The work of the pharmacist, once called a druggist, has evolved considerably from the days depicted on television or in the movies like *It's a Wonderful Life*, where the pharmacist would actually mix up a medication using powders and tinctures stored in boxes and bottles. Very little of this compounding is actually performed by a pharmacist anymore, as most medications are made in pharmaceutical factories in standard dosages. Instead, a pharmacist is responsible for dispensing prescription medications and explaining the nature of the medication, as well as dosage and side effects. While the doctor will have taken a history, including current medications, it is also the job of the pharmacist to advise on contraindications and interactions with other medications. To become a pharmacist, you have to graduate from an accredited college of pharmacy, pass the board examinations, and attain a state license.

The majority of pharmacists work in what are called community pharmacies, such as those in your local retail drugstore, hospital, or other health care facility. Some operate their own business, or work in a smaller independent shop that sells other health care supplies. In addition to dispensing medication and advising the patient on dosages and side effects, a pharmacist in a community pharmacy answers questions and offers advice on over-the-counter medications. Many also discuss such aspects of health as diet, exercise, and stress management, not only because these are important parts of overall wellness but also because improper management of any of the three can create the need for further medication. Some pharmacists provide services like blood-pressure testing, or programs to help those who are trying to quit smoking or better manage conditions like diabetes. A few even administer vaccinations. Beyond patient care, they often have paperwork such as third-party insurance forms to fill out, and liaise with prescribing doctors and pharmaceutical facilities.

> ## Essential Gear
>
> **Counseling skills.** Some patients have a closer relationship with their pharmacists than their doctors. Pharmacists tend to be more available, and you do not need an appointment to see one. You should be someone who welcomes this responsibility and handles it appropriately with strong counseling skills so that you gain and maintain patients' trust.

In addition to delivering medication and discussing it, pharmacists who work in hospitals or other health care facilities make sterile solutions for intravenous dosing and evaluate drug-pricing programs. Those who work in home health care also prepare injections.

A pharmacist can choose to specialize. Drugs like those used in oncology are complex and evolve regularly, so a specialist is often desirable in such an area. Other specialty subjects include geriatrics and psychiatry.

In tandem with the prescribing doctor, a pharmacist maintains computerized files on each patient's prescriptions. This helps to prevent harmful interactions and also allows a pharmacist to note if a drug is being taken longer than recommended.

New opportunities for pharmacists who may prefer a route outside retail include research in pharmaceutical companies, which entails the development and testing of new drugs. They can also work in marketing or sales, which puts them into contact with doctors and professional organizations, discussing new drugs and their uses. They also work for health insurance companies, performing cost-benefit analyses on drugs. Other employment opportunities are working for the government, HMOs, the military, or in a teaching or research facilities.

Because this field offers a good salary (many starting salaries are as high as $90,000), reasonable working hours, and job growth in the field, many people interested in health care are looking at pharmacy as an option. The education entails earning a Pharm.D. from an accredited college. The BS/MS option has been discontinued, so you must expect to spend four years earning your degree before spending a year in residency. Before applying, you must complete at least two years of college work, although three or more years is the norm. Requirements include mathematics, chemistry, organic chemistry, biology, physics, courses in social science, and sometimes public speaking. Communicating well with patients and doctors is a crucial aspect of being a good pharmacist. For most colleges, you must also successfully pass the Pharmacy College Admissions Test (PCAT).

Beyond learning all aspects of drug therapy and having solid communications skills, aspiring pharmacists study professional ethics, public health, and programs of drug distribution. They also work in practice settings under supervision. Upon completion of the degree, they then do at least one year of residency at a hospital or other clinical setting, although those wishing to specialize complete an additional year. Pharmacists who are especially interested in research or teaching go on to earn a Ph.D. in pharmaceutics, pharmaceutical chemistry, pharmacology, or pharmacy administration. Those who wish to run their own business also earn an MBA or degree in public administration or public health.

After the residency is completed, the pharmacist must then pass a series of exams to obtain a license, which is required by all the states. The exams vary by state, although all require the North American Pharmacist Licensure Exam, which tests skills and knowledge. There is also the

Multistate Pharmacy Jurisprudence Exam, and some states have their own exams. You will learn all about these requirements toward the end of your degree work. If you think you will be interested in practicing in more than one locality, you should investigate the requirements, as you may have to take an additional exam.

Although much of the workday is spent on your feet, and you may have to wear masks and gloves frequently because of contact with dangerous or sterile chemicals, you usually only work about 40 hours a week. However, many pharmacies are open 24 hours a day, seven days a week, so be prepared to work a number of nights and weekends as well as holidays. Thanks in part to the increased longevity in the geriatric population who tend to rely upon medications to maintain their good health, job opportunities are on the rise. Continued advances in drug development and a wider range of coverage by health insurance plans should also spur the demand for pharmacists. For those who have excellent math and science skills, as well as good communication and a genuine desire to serve the community, pharmacy might be your perfect Rx.

You Are Here

Determine if you have what it takes to be a pharmacist.

Do you have excellent scientific aptitude and math skills? Although you will not be mixing drugs yourself, you will be responsible for thoroughly understanding their contents and effects. You need to understand their chemical attributes, possible side effects, contraindications, allergy-related issues, and other aspects. As a pharmacist, you calculate doses and study patient profiles. Math is used in preparing formulas, chemical calculations, and determining weights and measures. A patient's weight and age is also taken into consideration for dosing. Generally, though, you match the script (prescription)—but in pharmacy accuracy, even for simple tasks, is no short order.

Do you have a strong memory and attention to detail? You need to keep details about hundreds of drugs in your brain, including their generic versions. You need to know what they do and what interactions they can have. Yes, you can look this up at any given time, but the more

Navigating the Terrain

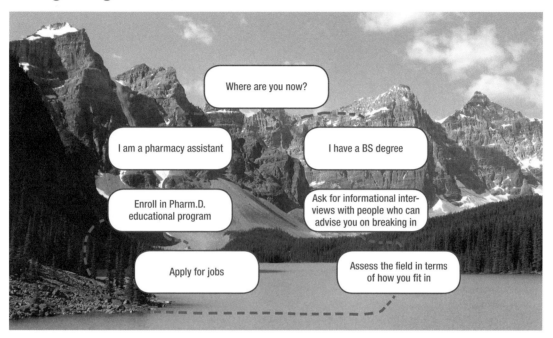

Where are you now?

I am a pharmacy assistant

I have a BS degree

Enroll in Pharm.D. educational program

Ask for informational interviews with people who can advise you on breaking in

Apply for jobs

Assess the field in terms of how you fit in

you remember, the better a pharmacist you will be. You also need to remember all you have learned and remain current with developments. Organizational skills and attention to detail are looked for in a new pharmacist. There is virtually no room for error when it comes to dispensing medication, and you want to be sure you have given the correct dosage and amount of pills every time.

Do you have a genuine interest in drugs and how they work? While the concerns that Americans are becoming too reliant upon chemical medications for all aspects of life, and doctors seem to be too quick to write a prescription when other forms of care might be warranted are all valid and important to review, a good pharmacist must still be interested in the abilities of drugs and what they can do. While it is the doctor who writes the prescription, a pharmacist often knows more about the drug, its contraindications, and possible interactions, especially depending upon what other conditions a patient might present. To maintain your

Stories from the Field

Leslie Adams, Pharm.D.
Pharmacist, Pharmacy Department, Clinical Center,
National Institutes of Health
Bethesda, Maryland

Leslie Adams came to pharmacy from an interest in biology and the desire for a career that would allow her to study drugs that could cure or manage human diseases. Upon completing her degree, she went on to a one-year residency at Johns Hopkins, which she admits is not a requirement for aspiring pharmacists, but a great step for those interested in working in a hospital, or choosing to specialize. Adams herself specializes in clinical research.

Her workday includes a number of activities, varying from liaising with members of the medical staff to answering questions and giving

license, you are required to continually learn about drug changes and developments, but to be a good pharmacist, you should want to do this anyway, regardless of requirements.

Organizing Your Expedition

Prepare yourself for the world of pharmaceuticals.

Develop strong interpersonal skills. As a pharmacist, you have a lot of patient contact. While it is not like the old days of the druggist on the corner who knows the whole neighborhood, you still need good communications skills to work closely with patients and be sure that they understand what their medication is, what it is for, and how to use it. If they are taking multiple medications, you must be able to help them develop a routine so that each drug is taken safely. You may face some communication challenges with people who speak different languages and come from diverse cultural backgrounds, but you must find a way to work with this. An episode of *ER* once showed a woman gravely ill because she only spoke and read Spanish. She read the word "once" on *information about medications to checking the dosages recommended by doctors to preparing the drugs themselves.*

Although Adams would like to incorporate direct patient care into her daily routine, she nonetheless derives a lot of satisfaction from being able to make a significant contribution to the work of the National Institutes of Health, which is dedicated to improving global human health through advances in science and research. She conducts investigations into drugs that may eventually be sanctioned for use by the Food and Drug Administration, thus immediately creating benefit for the population.

Adams is working toward her master's degree in public health with the goal of improving health care and access to underserved communities, thus hopefully closing the health gap between wealthier and poorer groups.

a prescription as the Spanish word for "11" and took the medication 11 times instead of just once. While dramatized for television, this is unfortunately an example of what can happen when the pharmacist does not work effectively with the patient or their family members to be sure they understand how to take their medication properly.

Be willing to accept responsibility. While it is usually a doctor who is targeted for a malpractice suit when something goes wrong, a pharmacist undertakes an immense responsibility. These professionals have many considerations when preparing a medication and a lot to communicate. Patients may not want to hear some of what you have to say. You have to accept this, but likewise, you have to be aware of how much is on your shoulders and be able to handle it.

Be sure you can separate your personal feelings from your profession. Recently, some pharmacists have been unwilling to fulfill prescriptions for certain medications because of their personal or political standpoints. Pharmacists study ethics as part of their degree, and some issues can be complex. Some pharmacists are also concerned about some doctors who may be writing unnecessary prescriptions. However, your job is to dispense medication. While you should certainly discuss a concern with a doctor if you have one, professional ethics call on you not to bring your personal beliefs behind the counter.

Learn about insurance administration and advocacy. Many pharmacists express concern and frustration with the problems of dealing with insurance companies. They can be overwhelmed with fussy paperwork, and this can impinge upon the time they have to spend with patients. Recent developments, like a radical increase in co-pay, has led to some patients being upset with pharmacists (rather than with their insurance companies). Those entering the field should be aware of these problems and develop skills for handling them. You may even make a positive difference in the lives of people who feel beleaguered by the health insurance system.

Landmarks

If you are in your twenties . . . If you are still in college, and especially if you are working on a BS, this is a good time to apply for a Pharm.D. If you do not mind spending another four to five years in education, you will have the reward of stepping into a very high-paying career before you are 30.

Essential Gear

Multitasking skills. As much time as you spend talking to patients and advising, you also have to be smart and fast and able to keep a lot going on at any one time. Whether you work in a retail or hospital pharmacy, a chain drugstore or your own business, you will likely be busy and have a lot to juggle. Under such circumstances, it is crucial that you be someone who can keep track of everything and do it all well.

If you are in your thirties or forties . . . If you have a strong science background, you might consider part-time schooling to get the necessary training. Schools are offering more part-time degree programs because the need for pharmacists is so high. Be upfront about your time needs with a school advisor, and you may be able to work out a course schedule that will allow you to continue working.

If you are in your fifties . . . If you have been working in another area of health care or as a pharmacy technician, you might be able to combine some work with your study, or use your skills or knowledge toward course credit.

If you are over sixty . . . Do not be intimidated by the four to five years you will have to spend learning how to do the job (or six, if you do not have any college credits already). The need for good pharmacists with excellent communication skills is high, and if you have a background that will apply, as well as excellent math and science skills, you will be a welcome applicant.

Further Resources

American Association of Colleges of Pharmacy The national organization representing schools of pharmacy and those who teach there. Check here for lists of accredited schools, information on application and financial aid and other resources. http.//www.aacp.org

American Society of Health-System Pharmacists A membership organization representing pharmacists who work in hospitals, other health care facilities, and home care. You can get information about education, advocacy, policies, and meetings. http://www.ashp.org

American Pharmacists Association The largest professional association of pharmacists in the country, the AphA is devoted to disseminating information, education, and advocacy. It offers information on drugs, government affairs, and meetings. http://www.aphanet.org

Veterinary Technician

Veterinary Technician

Career Compasses

Guide yourself to a career as a veterinary technician.

Relevant Knowledge of all aspects of animal health and wellness, as well as procedures and usage of equipment (40%)

Caring about the welfare of animals from birth to the possible need for euthanasia (30%)

Communication Skills to work effectively with team members and pet owners (20%)

Organizational Skills to maintain records and multitask (10%)

Destination: Veterinary Technician

One of the most important members of a veterinarian's support staff is the veterinary technician. The veterinary technician, or "vet tech," works alongside the veterinarian in providing high quality and human-grade care to animals, performing tasks such as operating X-ray machines, administering shots, restraining animals during difficult procedures, assisting in surgeries, suturing and dressing wounds, and advising pet owners on various issues of animal care. A good vet tech must, of course, love animals but also be aware that this can be a difficult job, with work that can be unpleasant, demanding, and occasionally even dangerous. For someone excited by these challenges, the career can be hugely satisfying.

In tandem with medical services for humans, veterinary medicine has advanced considerably in recent years. Better quality pet nutrition and wellness maintenance means that pets are living longer and healthier lives than ever before. Animal health issues such as geriatrics and obesity, previously only occasionally dealt with, are treated more and more. Pet owners and zoos expect top care, and as such, veterinary practices are expanding in kind with equipment and support staff. While vet techs work in a variety of settings, they are expected to perform routine lab and clinical procedures, usually under some supervision. Specifically, these include urinalysis, blood counts, dental care, taking blood samples, preparing tissue samples, and assisting in the use of machines involving test tubes and diagnostics.

Essential Gear

Attention to detail. You have to be very good at asking questions of owners and observing the animals. When giving shots, animals squirm or move, and you have to be exacting to jab them in exactly the right place each time. You want to notice small changes, slight irregularities, and any minor disruption under the coat or in the paw.

More often than not, it is the vet tech who takes patient histories, develops X-rays, and provides specialized nursing care. A more advanced vet tech discusses the pet's condition with the owners and even trains new hires.

The vast majority of vet techs deal predominately with cats and dogs, but aspirants should also be prepared to work with mice, rats, birds, turtles, rabbits, iguanas, snakes, and even fish. Vet techs also work with farm animals such as sheep, pigs, cattle, fowl, and horses. A zoo or aquarium's vet tech often specializes in a particular genus. Overall, a vet tech can expect to work in two main areas of animal care—either domestic companion animals or non-domestic animals. A rural vet tech may deal with both.

Vet techs who do not work in animal hospitals and veterinarians' offices or clinics may be integral to the staff of research facilities. Here, they administer medications, prepare lab samples, and record pertinent information. They may also work with lab and surgical equipment, administer vaccinations, provide basic postoperative care, and occasionally perform euthanasia. Most of this work is done under supervision or guidance.

Research work can also involve cloning and gene therapy in pursuit of health options for humans. Thus, vet techs might work in biomedical research, as well as wildlife medicine, livestock management, or various areas of pharmaceuticals.

While the opportunities are many and growing, the job can be difficult and stressful. The average veterinary office always smells of animals and can be very noisy, with barking and howling dogs and mewing cats. Even the most experienced vet tech must expect bites and scratches when lifting, holding, or restraining frightened or injured animals. Scrubs are regularly soiled with urine, feces, vomit, and blood. Vet techs often have to clean cages, which can be very messy. Precautions have to be taken when working with animals suffering rabies or who require treatment with germicides or insecticides.

Additionally, the job can entail a lot of emotional stress. While the business of having to euthanize a terminally ill animal can be hard, you at least have the satisfaction of knowing that the animal is no longer suffering. Although this is also true for unwanted or hopelessly injured animals, euthanizing is never routine for people who care deeply about animal health. Animal care workers who work in shelters, with rescue groups, or other human society organizations must regularly witness severe animal abuse and neglect. They often have to deal with owners who become hostile when confronted with an animal's condition. It can be difficult to remain calm and professional under such circumstances, but the job may require participation in enforcement proceeding so composure is a must.

The average vet tech's workweek will be about 40 hours, although some will work 50 or more. Additionally, animal medical needs arise 24/7, so some vet techs work occasional night or weekend duty.

A veterinary technology education has two programs. For veterinary technicians, a two-year program and successful passage of a state exam is all that is required. Someone interested in a job with higher pay and responsibility can undertake a four-year program, earning the title "veterinary technologist." Many veterinary technicians later complete this longer program to gain access to a wider range of job opportunities.

The veterinary technician program entails a two-year associate's degree earned at a community college accredited by the American Veterinary

Medical Association. Classes are taught in clinical and laboratory settings with live animals. The four-year program results in a bachelor's degree. Some schools offer distance learning, but of course the hands-on training is much more useful.

To qualify for entry into a program, an aspiring vet tech should have a solid background in science, biology, and math. Practical clinical skills are also useful. Many animal shelters, hospitals, and even private clinics have staff volunteers, which can be an excellent training ground. Once you have obtained your degree, the length of your period of on-the-job training before becoming credentialed is determined by how much hands-on experience you have undertaken with both the animals and the equipment used in the hospital.

To practice, you must have a license or certification, depending upon the state in which you work. All states require that you pass a credentialing exam, which involves oral, written, and practical sections, regulated by the state's board of veterinary examiners. Most states use the National Veterinary Technician exam. If you wish to work in research, you also have to gain certification from the American Association for Laboratory Animal Science.

Finally, prospective employers look for someone with excellent communication skills, a positive team attitude, good organizational skills, and a warm and caring touch.

You Are Here

Determine if you have what it takes to become a veterinary technician.

Do you have a lot of animal experience? While loving animals is key to doing good work in this field, you should also have some good basic experience. This will help you determine if you can handle some of the stressful aspects of the job. If you have had pets, have you administered medicine? It is relatively easy to give a dog a pill, because usually you just have to hide it in food, but giving even the calmest cats pills or liquid medication requires some skill and patience. Have you dealt with illness or injury? Have you performed home procedures in postoperative care? Have you experienced an emergency? If you have done any or all of these things and remained calm with a firm, sure touch, you may be an excellent candidate for vet tech work.

Navigating the Terrain

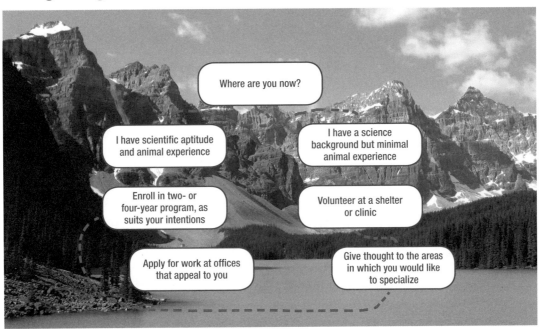

Where are you now?

I have scientific aptitude and animal experience

I have a science background but minimal animal experience

Enroll in two- or four-year program, as suits your intentions

Volunteer at a shelter or clinic

Apply for work at offices that appeal to you

Give thought to the areas in which you would like to specialize

Are you comparatively fearless? Puppies and kittens are lovely, but you will also have to deal with animals who are either poorly trained, unwell, or frightened, and they may growl and snap. It takes a particular kind of touch to manage a large, upset dog, and you cannot be the sort of person who shies from it. You must be someone who is firm, confident, and calm.

Do you have good people skills? While your patients may bite, scratch, or howl, it is often the people who come with them who can be the most difficult to deal with. Whether obstinate because they have not been taking proper care of their pets, or distraught because an animal is ill or injured, their needs will require your extra evenheadedness. For an animal that will require home treatment, you must clearly and patiently explain to the owner how to administer the treatment. Even loving owners can be nervous or careless in giving medications or other therapies. You must make sure they understand exactly what needs to be done and how to do it.

Notes from the Field
Mila M. Ballew
Licensed veterinary technician, Assistant technical director
Goose Creek, South Carolina

What were you doing before you got into veterinary work?

I was a wife and stay-at-home mom and I home-schooled my kids for several years.

Why did you decide to pursue veterinary work?

Both of my daughters were enrolled in school again and I felt it was time for me to prepare for the next phase of my life, which turned out to be working with animals.

What was involved in terms of education/training and getting your first job?

I signed up for classes at Trident Technical College and enrolled in the Veterinary Technology Program, which is a two-year degree. I needed to retake biology, since it had been more than five years since I'd last studied it. The other classes covered anatomy, radiology, psychology, ethics, anesthesiology, pharmacology, large animal, lab animal, and medical terminology, just to name a few. It was quite a transition for me, since I hadn't been in school for more than 20 years. I loved learning and won several scholarships and awards while at school. I also joined the National Association of Veterinary Technicians in America and the South Carolina Association of Veterinary Technicians when I started school,

Organizing Your Expedition

Prepare yourself for the woolly world of animal care.

Volunteer at a shelter or clinic. One of the best ways to determine if this is a job for you is to spend some serious time doing hands-on work and close observation at a shelter, clinic, or hospital. Besides that you will be doing a good deed because even the most well-funded animal shelters desperately need volunteers to help with feeding, cleaning, walking, organization, maintenance, and general aspects care. By volunteering you can get a real sense of what it is like to deal with a variety of animals in all stages of life and wellness every day. You may experience *which allowed me to get a real feel for the career. After my first year of classes, I started working part-time at a clinic for more experience.*

What are the keys to success in veterinary technician work?

You have to be willing to learn something new every day and have a powerful desire. I feel like I'm called to do this work. My daily job is never boring. Every day, I go home feeling like I made a difference, even if it is as simple as showing a client how to give a new puppy a nail trim, or explaining why heartworm prevention is so very important, or breathing for an animal that has crashed on the surgery table and then is brought back to life. This job allows you to make a difference in an animal's life and, very often, the owner's. I keep very busy—part of the time, I'm the surgery technician and the rest of the time, I work in the exam rooms. I do get a lot of wet kisses! To be really good at this, you must of course have a love for animals. Liking people also helps a lot. Animals don't carry wallets so you will always be dealing with a person. You have to have a desire to do your very best every day with every pet and every owner. You should be a high-energy, outgoing personality and be willing to take constructive criticism. You can always learn from someone else. One other important quality is the ability to separate yourself from the job at times. Performing euthanasia can be particularly hard. You need to realize that death is a part of life and many times, you are helping a bad situation get a bit better.

some sadness and anger at the lack of care and concern some humans exhibit toward animals. You can learn to channel those feelings into active care, some advocacy, and increased passion for the work of animal health maintenance. With experience volunteering at a shelter, clinic, or animal hospital, you will be well on your way to landing a good job.

Gauge your physical capacity. Carrying a terrier is one thing. But hefting an Irish wolfhound or St. Bernard onto a gurney or into a cage is something else. Most vet techs comment that it is less physical strength than stamina that is necessary to manage the work. If a cat escapes its cage, it can take a lot of effort and patience to retrieve it, and someone who has only had minimal dealings with cats may be surprised how wily they can be about being captured or placed in cages. You may also have to restrain a large animal for a long period of time. Unlike working with human patients, you cannot tell your animal patient what to do or how he or she can help you make both your lives easier. Treating animals requires a lot of energy and endurance.

Additionally, you want to be sure you have a strong stomach. Every day will see you dealing with a lot of urine and feces, including diarrhea, as well as blood and vomit. Emergencies and surgeries are not something everyone can handle, but you cannot keep a job as a vet tech unless you learn how. And while no one expects you to get "used to" euthanizing, it is unfortunately a regular and important part of the job.

Essential Gear

Good capacity for teamwork. A technician or technologist always works with colleagues and under the supervision of a veterinarian. Hiring veterinarians want to bring someone in who is committed to this teamwork environment. The turnover can be fairly high, which is understandable, given the pay opportunities, so you do well to convey a sense of commitment.

Be prepared for a possible pay cut. The good news is that employment opportunities are growing fast. Still, while the work is detailed, difficult, and entails a lot of responsibility, vet techs do not net the highest earnings. What you earn depends on your area and place of employment, as well as your education and training. A technologist earns more than a technician, but the wages are still not very high. The median hourly wage for a veterinary technician in 2006 was $12.88, according to the U.S. Bureau of Labor Statistics. As with a number of jobs in health care, this is a position you do more for personal satisfaction than high wages. Of course, you can always go on to get a degree as a full veterinarian, which will command a much higher salary.

Landmarks

If you are in your twenties . . . If you have grown up with animals, consider whether you would like to do the two- or four-year program and then go forward. You are in a good position to work as a vet tech for a few years and then transition to earning your degree as a full veterinarian.

If you are in your thirties or forties . . . If you are looking to supplement the family income with a job that will yield a lot of satisfaction, look for an accredited educational program in your area. If you live in a relatively urban area, employment prospects should be good, although it is useful to do some research beforehand.

If you are in your fifties . . . If you have some history of animal work, such as grooming, look into your ideal program while undertaking more extensive volunteer work in animal care. Your breadth of experience will help you secure a job with less training time and a slightly higher starting salary.

If you are over sixty . . . If you have a strong science background and good animal experience, you may want to limit yourself to looking for opportunities in animal research, where stamina is less of an issue than in hospitals, shelters, and clinics. Research facilities are always looking for people of steady character and good science knowledge and skills who will be devoted to the animals in their care.

Further Resources

National Association of Veterinary Technicians in America A membership organization with information on education, career development, leadership opportunities, publications, and current issues involving the work and animal wellness. http://www.navta.net

American Veterinary Medical Association While geared toward veterinarians, this is still a useful resource for finding accredited schools, current issues in animal health, publications, asking questions, and searching for jobs. http://www.avma.org

Association of Zoo Veterinary Technicians A membership organization offering externships and internships, job resources and other links, conference information, and assorted other resources. http://www.azvt.org

Physical Therapist

Physical Therapist

Career Compasses

Guide yourself to a career as a physical therapist.

Relevant Knowledge of the human body, injuries, and a range of exercises and stretches to improve health (30%)

Caring about the patient, no matter how difficult they may be, and their rate of progress (30%)

Communication Skills to work effectively with patients, family members, and other caregivers and medical professionals (20%)

Organizational Skills to maintain detailed files on every patient and balance more than one patient at a time in certain clinical settings (20%)

Destination: Physical Therapist

One of the fastest-growing and challenging-but-satisfying jobs in health care is that of physical therapist. As anyone who has ever suffered a serious injury knows, a physical therapist (PT) is the specialist who helps a person relieve pain and regain as much lost mobility and strength as possible or learn altogether new ways of functioning. People who have suffered accidents, as well as those with chronic back pain, arthritis, heart disease, bone fractures, and cerebral palsy are all treated by PTs.

When physical therapists first meet with a patient, they usually conduct their own history, in addition to reading the patient file beforehand. They then perform a series of tests to assess the patient's strength, mobility, balance, and coordination. Further tests examine posture, muscle and respiration capacity, and motor function. The PT then uses the test results to develop a treatment strategy and schedule. While PTs may have a sense of what the ultimate outcome of the treatment may be, they usually only discuss details of the treatment with the patient at this point, so as not to raise too many hopes in case the patient does not progress as well as they or the PT would like.

Essential Gear

Exercise equipment. While most modern facilities are well stocked with every necessity for good physical therapy, you will do well to spend some of your training time learning to master all of the equipment. Balance balls, treadmills, and devices for squeezing all require practice to handle. The better you know how to work with them, the more clearly you can communicate methods to your patients. You will also do better in designing individualized regimens.

The work of physical therapy predominately involves specially targeted exercises to help the patient regain strength and flexibility. The PT must develop exercises that work the areas around the injury so that those muscles are stronger and help support the injured area as it heals. The PT must also develop stretches and exercises that directly address the injury. The patients are involved in the healing process, performing exercises on their own at home and following the PT's advice on daily activities and posture so that the healing is expedited.

A physical therapist also uses equipment ranging from simple ice packs to electrical stimulation to ultrasound as part of the program of relieving pain and reducing swelling. Sometimes a PT employs traction or deep-tissue massage as a means of both relieving pain and improving circulation. If devices such as crutches, prostheses, or wheelchairs are needed, the PT instructs the patient in their use. Throughout the treatment process, the PT thoroughly documents the patient's progress and status while regularly undertaking further examinations for measuring statistics. Exercises and stretches are stepped up or altered as progress dictates.

While patients tend to be sent to a physical therapist when their work with an allopath is complete, the PT consults with the allopath at the beginning of treatment, and often reports progress. At any given time, depending on the patient's needs and treatment program, a PT also works with nurses, dentists, social workers, occupational therapists, speech-language pathologists, and audiologists.

To become a physical therapist, a person must earn a master's degree from an accredited program and a state license. The master's degree program typically lasts two years. You can also pursue a three-year doctoral degree. Coursework entails such science classes as biology, chemistry, and physics. Students then get more detailed with classes in biomechanics, neuroanatomy, human growth and development, disease manifestation, examination techniques, and therapeutic procedures. The coursework involves working in the laboratory and clinic, under strict supervision. A number of programs require you to have volunteered in a physical therapy capacity before they admit you as a student. You can gain such experience in a hospital, clinic, with a PT in private practice, or with a school's athletic trainer. This volunteer work serves a double purpose. It helps you determine if you really want to become a PT, and it gives you the opportunity to see if you have the personal, as well as practical, qualifications. A successful PT must have strong interpersonal skills to discuss the treatment procedure with the patient and patient's family, as well as a vast store of patience, compassion, and desire to help. Many of the patients who come to physical therapy are despondent and concerned about their ability to regain their full health. A good PT must give them confidence while not selling them false hope. Rather, it is important to encourage a patient and remain practical and focused.

While you do not have to have a science background to pursue an MA in physical therapy, some educational work in anatomy, biology, chemistry, social science, math, and physics can help.

For a physical therapist to remain successful, he or she must realize that education does not end with the awarding of a degree. A PT is expected to keep up-to-date with developments in the field by attending regular conferences, courses, and workshops. In some states, a PT who fails to continue education in this way will not have his or her license renewed.

Physical therapists can work in a hospital, clinic, or private office. Likewise, they can treat a range of ailments or specialize. Some specialties include pediatrics, geriatrics, orthopedics, sports medicine, neurology, and cardiopulmonary physical therapy. Although the job is all about helping people regain their physical health, the work itself is physically taxing. A PT spends the day stooping, kneeling, or crouching while helping patients stretch and exercise. There is heavy equipment that continually needs shifting and adjusting, and even the lightest patients become heavy when the PT is bearing all their weight to help them turn, stand, or walk. Many PTs practice Pilates, yoga, or swim in order to keep their own muscles and posture in top condition so that they can continue to perform their job.

While physical therapists find a lot of employment opportunities, an aspiring PT should be aware that nearly one in five work part-time, and many have a job in a hospital as well as a clinic. A PT, especially in private practice, must at least some evenings and weekends to accommodate patient schedules. It should also be noted that the median wage, while solid, is not as large as wages in some other areas. Someone transitioning from a position in a corporate or technological environment is likely to experience a pay decrease. However, the need for physical therapists is growing exponentially with the aging of the baby boom population and general poor health of large segments of the society, so wages are likely to increase in time.

Most of the patients treated by physical therapists improve to at least some degree, which is part of why many physical therapists experience a high level of job satisfaction. If the idea of working one-to-one with a patient to help him or her regain health appeals, you should certainly explore the fast-growing world of physical therapy.

You Are Here

Do you have the requisite strong backbone for physical therapy?

Are you enthused about the idea of working with patients one-on-one? While many medical professionals work closely with patients, a physical therapist is involved more closely for a longer amount of time than almost any other health care professional except for a home care nurse. In this job, you work with someone for an hour at a time, anywhere from once a week to every day, from a few weeks to over a year. You have to deal with a range of personalities and problems, both in the

Navigating the Terrain

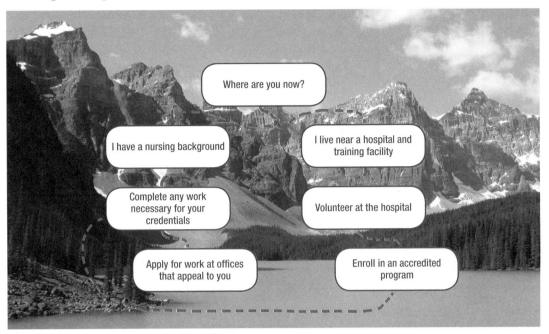

Where are you now?

I have a nursing background

I live near a hospital and training facility

Complete any work necessary for your credentials

Volunteer at the hospital

Apply for work at offices that appeal to you

Enroll in an accredited program

patients and their families. People may be depressed if they feel they are not making progress, and they may take their frustrations out on you. Likewise, if a patient is not doing his or her part by performing exercises and stretches at home, you might become frustrated with them. It takes a lot of patience to work.

Do you understand the particular problems of the elderly? Unless you specialize in pediatrics or sports medicine, many of your patients will be elderly. As the baby boomers have aged, the need for good physical therapists in hospitals, clinics, and private practice has surged. Many in this population can be particularly challenging to work with, especially if they have other illnesses or some mental degeneration. (Many, too, make for distinctly pleasurable clients—as with any population, personality is everything.) Some younger physical therapists have found that, because they are not referred to as "doctor," a few older patients are less likely to listen to their recommendations. You have to learn to work

Notes from the Field

Alissa Telchin
Physical therapist
Philadelphia, Pennsylvania

What were you doing before you decided to change careers?

I had majored in biology as an undergrad and was so burnt out, I couldn't handle med school, so I took a job in the manufacturing lab of a diagnostic company. We made test kits for STDs, HIV/AIDS, and the like. I knew I was helping people, but I wanted to feel like I was doing more, and I wanted to use my science degree.

Why did you change your career?

What I was doing wasn't helping enough, but I was uncertain about med school because HMOs pressured doctors to spend less time with patients, and I wanted to spend a lot of time with them and not be pressured about billing. I happened to hurt my wrist and needed physical therapy. Since it was just a hand injury, I had to sit at a table and do exercises and got to watch the PTs work with everyone else. It seemed more of what I wanted . . . no desk, work with people, use your brain, solve problems. At first, I wasn't sure I could emotionally detach enough, especially with the older patients, having dealt with very sick grandparents. I did some observation at my local hospital and found I could deal. And when I talked to the PT afterwards, everything he said about what he liked in the work clicked. I always said I'd know my dream job when fireworks went off, and they did.

with these patients and their family members and caregivers in a way that grants everyone, including yourself, respect.

Are you a good listener? To be a good physical therapist, you need to work well with a number of other specialists and pay close attention to their prognoses and concerns. And you also need to pay careful attention to your patient. Sometimes you have to find a way to adapt the main doctor's recommendations to the patient's abilities due to their work and lifestyle. This requires listening carefully to both of them and developing your own therapies accordingly..

How did you make the transition?

I determined what schools I wanted to apply to and what classes I still needed to take, as well as how much volunteer time I would have to put in. Then I quit my job and took the prereqs at a community college while volunteering and applying to schools. The adjustment to school was hard because the classes are intense in the first year. I had been out of school for a few years and had to get back in the study mood and learn to balance social life and school again.

What are the keys to success in your career?

In terms of doing well in school, I found that volunteering in more than one setting helped me get a job while I was still in school—I got a job as a PT aide in an outpatient clinic, which was good because I felt it all sank in more. You don't learn a lot of exercises in school, and I could better understand why a PT did something with a patient in this setting. There are some schools that have programs called "externships," which is an extension of the clinical experience and a work-study job. That was great, because I was getting paid to learn and sometimes I would learn something in class and then see it in the hospital the next day. Do your research for schools well. Ask them about their retention rate for graduation and the amount of TAs they have. (For first-year classes you need more than one professor to ten students.) One thing I like is that you're always teaching. You teach your patients what's going on with them and what to do. And there are a lot of settings—outpatient, inpatient acute care, inpatient rehabilitation, women's health, cardiac, etc. It is kind of like nursing in that degree, but you don't have to deal with blood or poo that much.

Organizing Your Expedition

Be sure you have everything you need as you set out on the road to physical therapy.

Determine if you would like to specialize. As noted, a number of specialties are available for an aspiring physical therapist. The aging population may inspire you to specialize in geriatrics. If you have an athletic background, you may be more inclined toward sports medicine. If you have worked in nursing in an orthopedics or neurological arena, this may be a natural transition. For veterans of parenting looking to get into physical therapy, pediatrics may be the perfect fit. The choice to specialize is not so easy as one might think because the needs in the job market are constantly shifting, so with the one exception of geriatrics, you can possibly have a harder time landing a good job in a place that feels like a good fit. You may have to be prepared to make compromises, including working with a wider range of patients or relocating.

Scout your particular terrain. While more than 200 accredited programs in physical therapy are available in this country, if you do not live near one, you will have to move once you are accepted. And unless your degree program is in a major metropolitan area, you may have to move again once you have completed your education, depending upon where you are offered work. This can be fine, and even exciting, for people in their twenties, but if you are settled in an area and have a family, it might be more daunting. Consult with the physical therapists at your local hospital about education and job possibilities within a comfortable commuting range before you begin applying for programs.

Essential Gear

Back brace. This is for you, not the patients. While you work hard to maintain your own good condition, the amount of lifting and shifting you will have to will be tiring. A good back brace, such as that worn by weight lifters or furniture movers, will help you prevent any injury to yourself. Your job is to treat, not be treated.

Be prepared to spend less time with your family and friends. The first year of coursework in becoming a physical therapist is intense, even for those with a science background. You may have to sacrifice other obligations, including social time, in order to keep up. It will get easier, and once you become a PT you can work a fairly normal, 40-hour week schedule, but the work involved in earning your MA will be grueling.

Get in your own best physical condition. This is not a requirement and no one is suggesting you become a top athlete or supermodel, but being a physical therapist can be as demanding on the body as working in construction. You are constantly putting your own body in awkward positions in order to help your patients learn how to use their body properly, either again or for the first time. A lot of lifting and supporting needs to be done, and sometimes you have to catch someone before they fall and re-injure themselves. This is all taxing on your body. Add to that the increasing rates of obesity in the country, and you may find yourself dealing with many patients, even children, who are heavy for their frames. The obese are often in need of physical therapy as their bodies become unwieldy. If they are unaccustomed to regular exercise, they will need more attention so they can be trained to improve their daily regimen. It can all be very physically hard on the PT, so the better shape you are in and the more you understand about your own body and its abilities, the better work you will do.

Landmarks

If you are in your twenties . . . If you do not have family obligations, take your time researching your ideal MA program, because location should not be a consideration at this point. Look for a program that is highly rated and will allow you to participate in various communities to gain a wide range of experience.

If you are in your thirties or forties . . . Look for good volunteer opportunities to help you determine if this is something you really want to do. Consult with the physical therapists on staff about programs that might be flexible, have a good retention rate, and might put you in a position to get work in a location of your choosing.

If you are in your fifties . . . Volunteer at a nursing home or similar sort of rehabilitation center and consult on MA programs there. Some hospitals will have teaching facilities and you might be able to parlay your volunteer work into an educational opportunity.

If you are over sixty . . . If you have experience in nursing or working with children, consider focusing on a specialty in pediatrics. Likewise, it is understood that someone with a long experience of dealing with children will have stores of patience and abilities that someone younger may not have.

Further Resources

American Physical Therapy Association A membership organization discussing education, advocacy, research, legal issues, and a host of other topics pertinent to the field. It also has information for the public, legislators, and other health-care professionals. http://www.apta.org

American Academy of Physical Therapy A nonprofit organization dedicated to helping minorities and those who are financially disadvantaged to pursue careers in health professions. Also works to improve access to care for disadvantaged members of society. http://www.aaptnet.org/home

Physical Therapy Resources   A list of Internet resources compiled by the Health Science and Human Services Library at the University of Maryland. http://www.hshsl.umaryland.edu/resources/physicaltherapy.html

Dental Hygienist

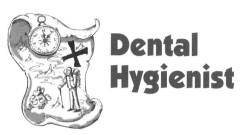

Dental Hygienist

Career Compasses

Guide yourself to a career as a dental hygienist.

Relevant Knowledge of tools, procedures, and equipment (30%)

Caring about all aspects of your patients' health, as this impacts their oral health (25%)

Communication Skills to teach patients good oral health techniques and help them get enthusiastic about maintaining proper oral hygiene (25%)

Organizational Skills to keep to a schedule and manage all necessary tasks, as well as handle emergencies (20%)

Destination: Dental Hygienist

From the evil dentist in *Little Shop of Horrors* to any number of mostly stupid jokes, dentists are often unjustly portrayed. People who deal in teeth for a living have enough to contend with in their daily job. A good sense of humor about the work is necessary, especially because the realities can often be frustrating, depending on where you work and your patient base. Despite improvements in toothbrushes, toothpaste, dental floss, and other home tools to maintain good oral hygiene, the average dental hygienist confronts a lot of plaque, tartar, red gums, and bad breath because of high-sugar diets and poor oral hygiene habits. This is one of the fastest-growing jobs in the country, with continued excellent prospects, according to the U.S. Bureau of Labor Statistics. Plus, most of the work environments are pleasant and flexible with very good to excellent pay.

Anyone who has been to the dentist for his or her yearly cleaning and checkup knows what hygienists do. They are the ones who do the cleaning. Specifically, a dental hygienist removes the hard and soft deposits from the teeth, performs a basic examination of the teeth and gums, records conditions to be discussed with the dentist prior to examination, and instructs the patients in the healthy maintenance of their teeth.

Cleaning teeth requires the use of a number of tools. First, the hygienist uses a mirror to perform a basic visual assessment of the teeth, noting buildup of plaque and tartar and possible abnormalities. Then the hygienist employs a series of metal scrapers to manually remove the tartar and plaque. For a patient with poor oral hygiene, this can take a long time. Dental professionals rely on manual dexterity, care, and wrist stamina. In addition to hand tools, the hygienist uses rotary and ultrasonic instruments to clean and then polish the teeth. The normal cleaning session is finished with flossing by hand and then a review of basic home maintenance techniques.

Other work includes removing stains, taking X-rays, and sometimes developing the X-rays. A hygienist must be personable as well as efficient. For example, the plastic bites a patient must hold between his or her teeth during the X-ray process can be uncomfortable and sometimes trigger the gag reflex, so hygienists have to move fast and be reassuring. In some states, hygienists can be licensed to administer anesthetics. They may also be allowed to place and carve filling materials, temporary fillings, and periodontal dressings. Additionally, they may remove sutures and smooth and polish metal restorations. They may make some diagnoses and can prepare clinical and diagnostic tests.

The bulk of the job, however, entails working with patients. You clean their teeth and then discuss with them how to develop or maintain good home oral care, including issues such as selecting a toothbrush, bristle strength, the advantages of handheld versus electric brushes, and mouthwash. You discuss various kinds of floss and demonstrate the best flossing techniques. You also have to talk about things a lot of patients will not want to hear, such as dietary choices that may be affecting oral health. This can be especially difficult when working with adolescents or the parents of small children who do not want to make any changes in their diets. While most people understand that sodas and even some fruit juices are full of sugars and other chemicals that can wreak havoc upon teeth and possibly lead to more serious health problems, few people like to be told that they should cut down on something they enjoy or to which they are addicted. Along with a lot of patience and understanding, a warm, pleasant manner and inventive educational techniques are handy for good dental hygiene work.

Most of a dental hygienist's work takes place in a clean, quiet office. Hygienists follow a number of important safeguards, such as the use of gloves, surgical masks, and safety glasses, as well as protective and special gear for working with X-rays or anesthesia. Some dental hygienists participate in community service programs, so that once or twice a year, they might perform cleanings on patients in nursing homes, mental hospitals, or prisons, always with appropriate safety measures in place.

Essential Gear

Manual dexterity. This need cannot be emphasized enough. If you do not have good dexterity, you will not be awarded your degree. People who play piano or guitar are excellent candidates, but you can also improve your dexterity through hand and finger exercises. Squeezing foam balls, learning card and coin tricks, and performing other exercises all help. You learn a few tricks in school, but the more you can do to get and keep your fingers nimble, the better.

One of the biggest advantages touted by dental hygienists is the job's flexibility. More than half of hygienists work part-time, and a variety of schedules are available, making it an ideal job for parents with young children, for example.

Becoming a dental hygienist requires earning a degree from an accredited school of dental hygiene. This can take anywhere from two to four years, depending on what requirements you have already fulfilled and what sort of degree you would like to earn. Most accredited programs require that you have a high school diploma and have done moderately well in math, chemistry, biology, and English. Dental hygiene training programs ask for college entrance test scores, and many want you to have completed at least one year of college work, either toward an associate's or bachelor's degree. You may also have to fulfill core educational prerequisites in chemistry, English, speech, psychology, and sociology. Some schools ask for an interview, dexterity test, or essay. The two-year program yields an associate's degree, or diploma or certificate, while the four-year ends with a bachelor's degree. Some hygienists choose to go on to a master's degree, and then teach, pursue research, or advance to administration. All programs require an average of 1,948 "clock hours," which includes 585 hours in clinical work under supervision. You must also study humanities, sciences such as anatomy, microbiology, pathology, and nutrition, and specific dental courses, including head and neck anatomy, oral pathology, radiography, periodontology, and pain control. Training covers preventive counseling, clinical dental hygiene, community dental health, patient management, and dental emergencies, as well as legal and ethical issues. Finally, you will be supervised in clinical work. Upon receiving your degree, you then have to take an exam to earn your license. The exam is set by the American Dental Association's Joint Commission on National Dental Examinations and includes written and clinical portions.

Dental hygienists are very much in demand, so if you like the idea of working with people and their teeth, and have good science and people skills, you could find yourself embarking on a fun new career in as little as two years.

You Are Here

Determine if you have what it takes to be a dental hygienist.

Do you have excellent eye-hand coordination and manual dexterity?
Much of this job involves using sharp objects inside a patient's mouth, so there is not much space for error. If you slip, you can pierce the gum, lip, or tongue. You must be prepared for unexpected patient movement, be able to anticipate, and be confident in your dexterity. You must also be able to gauge your pressure, so that you are using just enough to successfully remove plaque and other debris, but not so much so that you are putting undue pressure upon the teeth, gums, or patient. Many patients are uncomfortable with dental procedures, so they complain even during a routine cleaning. You must learn to figure out how to perform your duties to keep these complaints to a minimum.

Do you have excellent communication skills and work well with others? Dental offices can be small and intimate so that you may be working closely with a dentist, one or two other hygienists, a dental assistant, and perhaps a receptionist. Much of your work is done beside the dentist or dental assistant, so you must be an integral, effective team member. Additionally, the close work you do with patients, whose backgrounds and educations span a wide range, requires that you be a warm, friendly, and effective communicator.

Are you organized, efficient, and able to keep to a schedule? Although the hours are flexible, time on the job is not. Patients arrive late and may have a lot more plaque to scrape off than you expected, which can wreak havoc with a busy office schedule. You have to be an efficient worker who can do a thorough cleaning and try to get things back on track without skipping out on anything necessary. You will have a lot to keep track of during the day, with X-rays, surgeries, and cleanings, and you have to be someone who can manage it all, plus handle emergencies as they arise.

Navigating the Terrain

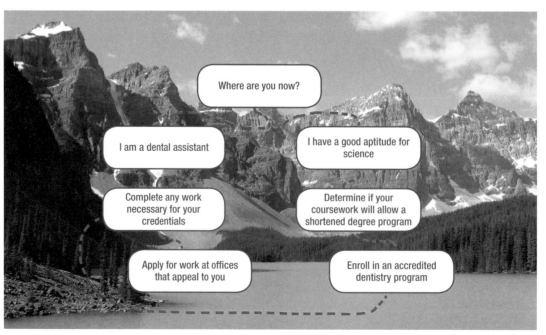

Where are you now?

I am a dental assistant

I have a good aptitude for science

Complete any work necessary for your credentials

Determine if your coursework will allow a shortened degree program

Apply for work at offices that appeal to you

Enroll in an accredited dentistry program

Organizing Your Expedition

Prepare yourself to become a dental hygienist.

Become a student of human psychology. While you take psychology courses as part of learning to become a dental hygienist, it is useful to learn more on your own. Much of this job involves education and a kind of counseling. You deal with a wide variety of patients from a number of backgrounds and not all of them have been to a dentist with any regularity or taught the intricacies of maintaining good oral hygiene. You also need to be someone who can take the entire person into account, rather than just focus on their mouth. The whole of someone's medical history and lifestyle factors into the state of their oral hygiene, and the more you understand, the better you are able to work with them and guide them.

Essential Gear

Patience. Dental hygienists, perhaps more than many other health care professionals, come up against stubborn patients. For people who have been brushing their own teeth since they were three or four, they are sure they know how and do not need to be taught. They certainly do not want to hear that they are not doing the best job. You have to accept that they may not make positive changes, but you also have to keep encouraging them. Help them consider the value of good oral health to overall wellness.

Sharpen your preventative care education techniques. Among the reasons for the increased demand for quality dental hygienists is that older people are retaining more of their teeth. Also, dental professionals and the population at large are placing more focus on preventative care. It was not so long ago that most people expected to have not just one, but probably a few, fillings by the time they were 18. And up till the postwar period few people had any expectation of keeping all their teeth past the age of 60. Improvements in toothbrushes, toothpaste, floss, and education have made enormous changes. People are actively interested in keeping their teeth healthy and looking their best. Your job is to make sure that they understand how to brush and floss properly and how to supervise their children's brushing and flossing. Many people think it is something they do not need to be taught, but many people also do not know the proper techniques. You have to teach them without condescension or criticism.

Notes from the Field

Jean Connor, RDH
President, American Dental Hygienists' Association
Cambridge, Massachusetts

What were you doing before you decided to become a dental hygienist?

I worked for about 10 years as a dental assistant early in my early twenties. Then I left dentistry and started working in sales, which included selling spring water, and then switched to communication (pagers, voicemail systems etc).

Why did you decide to pursue a career as a dental hygienist?

In the early nineties, I realized that [sales] was not what I would like for a lifelong career and wanted to look at what I could do to make a great salary while enjoying what I would do every day. I looked back to my years in dentistry and decided to apply to dental hygiene schools. Health care is a great field for growth and stability, and I really enjoyed my time as a dental assistant.

What was involved in terms of education/training and landing your first job?

When I applied to my selected program, I was too late for the incoming class. This led me to apply for a health program where I took courses that could be applied to the dental hygiene program.

Make them feel that they are a part of the team effort in keeping their teeth in good order. With your younger patients especially, you want to get them excited about keeping teeth healthy.

Know the variety of toothpaste and whitening ingredients. As part of maintaining healthy teeth, more adults are turning to whiteners that are available at any drugstore. Many of these actually do a decent job, without any harm to the teeth, but with so many products coming out so quickly, some have problematic ingredients. Dental organizations work hard to keep tabs on what is on the market, and you should as well, so that you can advise patients.

While in school, I joined the American Dental Hygienists' Association as a student member and was selected to attend the annual national meeting as a student representative. I met many hygienists from across the country as well as many from my home state. Through these contacts, I was able to find opportunities for my first job, and all subsequent positions. During my dental hygiene career, I have practiced in many different scenarios. I have worked for temporary agencies that place you in different offices, small offices with only you and one dentist, and now I am in an office with 10 dentists and eight hygienists, all with different specialties. My dental hygiene education brought me to a job working as a health care investigator. After earning additional certification as an investigator, I worked for the state dental board investigating complaints against dentists and hygienists advocating for patients.

What are the keys to success in this career?

I feel that the key to success, and long-term career satisfaction is to be connected to the American Dental Hygienists' Association. The continuous changes occurring in health care, and the desire to stay on the "cutting edge" of technology—and to be the best I can be—requires continued lifelong learning. The American Dental Hygienists' Association is the best resource for this education, as well as changes in the scope of practice and expanding opportunities for dental hygienists.

Landmarks

If you are in your twenties . . . If you are interested in a career where you can help people but have time to explore other interests, you should start researching accredited schools of dental hygiene now. If you decide you like the work and wish to advance, you will have plenty of time to either earn a master's in the field or transition to being a full dentist.

If you are in your thirties or forties . . . If you are looking for something that will allow you to give a lot of time to manage family obligations while earning good money and being a positive enforcer of health maintenance, the two-year option is perfect. Determine if you need to fulfill any prerequisites before you begin applying to accredited programs.

If you are in your fifties . . . You may want to bone up on the science and humanities requirements before applying to accredited programs, just to prime yourself for the science education ahead.

If you are over sixty . . . If you have a lifelong interest in science, you should definitely apply to the two-year program. The demand for good hygienists is high and offices will be eager to hire someone who knows their stuff and is looking to stay in that job for a while.

Further Resources

American Dental Hygienists' Association A membership organization that offers information on education, continuing education, developments in oral hygiene, publications, and other resources. http://www.adha.org
American Dental Association The largest organization of oral health professionals, its Commission on Dental Accreditation can be useful in the search for accredited schools of dental hygiene, as well as additional information and resources. http://www.ada.org
State Dental Associations Individual states have their own professional associations. Consult your local chapter for information on job searching, licensing, and other questions or concerns you may have.

Optician

Optician

Career Compasses

Guide yourself to a career as an optician.

Relevant Knowledge of tools, procedures, and equipment (30%)

Mathematical Skills to perform precision measurements and cut lenses based on geometric and physics principles (30%)

Communication Skills to work with customers to help them find the eyewear that best suits their needs (20%)

Organizational Skills to keep good customer records and run a business (20%)

Destination: Optician

With computers, video iPods, and mobile phones, it is a wonder that the entire population of this electronics-addicted world does not need corrective eyewear. Still, more and more do, increasing the need for good opticians.

The title *optician* can be somewhat deceptive because people who operate retail dispensing shops can be called "opticians" even though they are not licensed professionals. However, 22 states do require that even a dispensing optician be licensed; and whereas this was once solely a profession learned on the job or via a two-year apprenticeship, more re-tailers want a candidate to have undergone postsecondary education in opticianry. No matter how they came to earn their credentials, they are still regulated by governing boards.

An optician builds corrective lenses based upon a prescription from an ophthalmologist or optometrist. These can be contact lenses, glasses, low-vision aids, or ophthalmic prosthetics. The optician works with the client to determine what device is best for his or her needs and lifestyle. Many people are very sensitive about their need for corrective eyewear and want to be sure that they do not have to compromise their look and style in order to see clearly. The optician helps them select and fit eyeglasses, or contact lenses based on the needs of the pre-scription and the wearer. Things like work, lifestyle, and habits must be taken into consideration. Once all this has been discussed and a recommendation made, the fitting can begin. If the person is going to get glasses, the optician measures their eyes and the dis-tance between the centers of the pupils and the distance between the ocular surface and the lens. This all leads to the perfect pair of specs.

Essential Gear

The latest in facial safety wear. Whether you run your own business or are part of a large operation, you want to make sure that the most state-of-the-art safety wear is available. You will be working with glass, cutting machinery, and chemicals. None of it will pose any real hazards if you are properly protected every time you sit down to work with it.

Some people need new glasses and come to a dispensing optician with their old glasses in hand, but not a copy of the original prescrip-tion. In this instance, the optician uses a measuring instrument called a *focimeter*, which can help duplicate the existing lenses. The optician can also contact the optometrist or ophthalmologist who wrote the prescrip-tion to get more information. Some opticians even work in a joint prac-tice with optometrists or ophthalmologists, which creates convenience for patients and practitioners alike.

On the whole, however, most opticians work independently from the eye doctors. Workplaces can vary from retail shops to independent of-fices, hospitals, or eye care centers. With people living longer and more people needing corrective eyewear sooner, the job opportunities are growing apace.

Becoming a licensed optician does not take very long. You must have a GED or high school diploma and then complete an accredited optician program. In 2007, there were 21 accredited degree programs authorized by the Commission on Opticianry Accreditation. By completing one of these one- to two-year programs, you earn a certificate, diploma or associate's degree. Those who excel in opticianry school often have a good grounding in science and math, which is crucial for the coursework. Classes include physics, biology, anatomy, algebra, geometry, trigonometry, geometrical optics, and ophthalmic optics. Potential opticians also receive training with various instruments and tools that are part of the daily work. Computer skills are also valuable. If you are interested in running your own business, you should take some courses in management and administration.

Professionals learn a great deal of the skills on the job. Depending on the employer, you either enter into a formal apprenticeship or simply receive on-the-job training under supervision. The job itself is fairly comfortable, with the hours usually at about 40 per week. Opticians in retail stores should expect to work some nights and weekends. The job poses few potential hazards, but opticians take extra care working with glass cutting machinery and chemicals.

Essential Gear

Fashion magazines. You do not just want to show customers you are up on the latest trends in eyewear, you actually want to know what is hot. Keep magazines geared toward a breadth of consumers in varying age and income groups and be sure to bookmark Web sites for yourself that discuss fashion trends. Even customers whom you think will not care what the latest style is might be interested in something trendy, and you should be able to discuss it with them.

In the 22 states that require you obtain a license before practicing, you have to pass a practical exam, written test, and a certification test under the auspices of the American Board of Opticianry (ABO) and the National Contact Lens Examiners (NCLE). Most states require that you work as an apprentice for anywhere from two to four years before you are deemed eligible to sit for the licensing exams, although some allow recent graduates of accredited programs to take the exams after completion of their education. You will be expected to take continuing education courses in order to qualify for license renewal.

Additionally, an optician may apply to the ABO and NCLE to receive certification, irrespective of state requirements. Certification is a nationally recognized credential that indicates to customers and employers alike that you have attained an acknowledged and measurable level of expertise, which can improve your prospects for work and salary, as well as put clients at their ease. To remain certified, you must take continuing education courses and renew your certificate every three years.

Even a certified optician will not do well, however, without excellent people skills. The job is less a specific health care profession than a service, and opticians work closely with people to help them select eyewear that suits their taste and price range. As an optician, you have to educate customers in eyeglass maintenance or contact lens insertion and care. If you are operating your own business, much of your work will come via referrals from eye doctors and client word of mouth, so while you absolutely must be skilled and knowledgeable, you also have to be someone people want to see for their eyewear needs again and again. So if you want to work fairly independently, run a business, and provide a necessary and important service, opticianry may be for you.

You Are Here

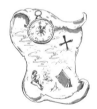

See if you are a good fit for opticianry.

Are you dexterous and well-coordinated? Your math and science abilities may be top-notch, as are your personal skills, but a good optician must also have excellent manual dexterity. Besides handling complex machinery, you will be doing a lot of precision work in this field. You often have to mend or reset frames and do minute adjustments. An entire day may be spent making precision measurements, and there is almost no room for error. You have a number of tools to assist you, but you still need to depend on sensitive and strong fingers.

Do you enjoy physics and geometry? Being good at math and science and actually enjoying the disciplines are two different things. If you have always been the sort of person who genuinely loved experiments and working with planes and spatial problems, it follows that you will probably enjoy carving out lenses and measuring them for accuracy and weight.

Do you wear corrective eyewear yourself? By no means a requirement or even necessity, the first-hand experience of using eyewear can be an asset in the trade. Customers certainly take notice of it and may regard you as more of an "equal." Many people who need glasses or even contact lenses for the first time are uncomfortable and feel awkward discussing their concerns and desires in terms of look and practicality. If you wear stylish glasses yourself, or are an old hand with inserting contact lenses, customers may feel more comfortable engaging with you and trusting you to help them select the eyewear that will work for them.

Organizing Your Expedition

Prepare yourself to become an optician.

Study eyes and faces. While you will learn eye anatomy and facial measurement in school, really understanding how frames and lenses look on an individual involves having a strong, almost artistic, sense of the face. Many people like the idea of lightly tinted spectacles lenses, or colored contact lenses. You will be able to advise and guide them if you can perceive how the color they are leaning toward will work with their eyes. You will gain a reputation as a good optician if you can guide people toward frames that enhance their features and even add to their attractiveness. Someone may want a particular trendy frame, but if you can see that it will not work for them and instead steer them to something unexpected but flattering, the customer may well remember and refer others. A little consideration goes a long way.

Learn how to teach. For people new to the wearing of corrective lenses, the learning curve can be unexpected. Many assume they simply put on their new glasses or insert their contact lenses and then get on with their daily routine. They will not necessarily realize that contact lenses can feel like manhole covers on the eyes at first and take as long as a few weeks to be comfortable enough to wear all day and night. Even the lightest frames exert some pressure on the ears and bridge of the nose initially, which may be exacerbated if the weather is hot or humid. Additionally, although people see better with eyewear, the change is still

Navigating the Terrain

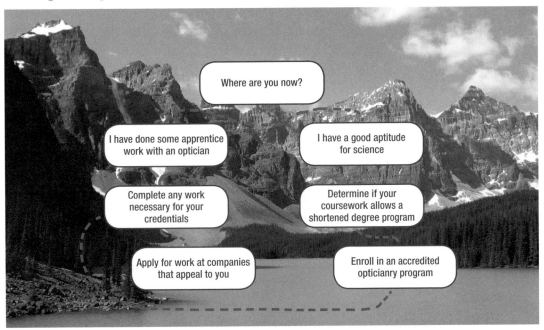

Where are you now?

I have done some apprentice work with an optician

I have a good aptitude for science

Complete any work necessary for your credentials

Determine if your coursework allows a shortened degree program

Apply for work at companies that appeal to you

Enroll in an accredited opticianry program

disconcerting at first and takes some getting used to. Share tips if you have them for making the adjustment more comfortable.

Maintain your manual dexterity via hand exercises. If you play a musical instrument like the piano or guitar, you already have excellent dexterity, which helps considerably when working with needle-nose pliers to make minute adjustments in frames. Squeezing foam balls and learning coin and card tricks, or specific hand and finger exercises, especially combined with eye-hand coordination exercises, helps for work with precision machinery.

Landmarks

If you are in your twenties . . . If you have a GED or equivalent plus a bit of solid, postsecondary coursework in math and science, you are a good candidate for the one- to two-year program and apprenticeship. You should also consider getting a certificate, as customers and employers

Notes from the Field

Donna M. Sims
Optician, University Health Services
Hadley, Massachusetts

What were you doing before you became an optician?

I spent a long time working two jobs as a waitress and a window cleaner. My son was 10 years old, and I was a single mom trying to make ends meet.

Why did you decide to become an optician?

I have always been interested in eye care, although I didn't get the chance to pursue it earlier on. My interest comes from a difficult place because there is a history of eye disease in my family—my father has been legally blind since I was a baby.

What was involved in terms of education/training and getting your first job?

I found out that Holyoke Community College was offering a two-year certificate program for opticianry, and that it was being federally

may not feel confident entrusting their eyewear to someone so young, and the certification evidences your training.

If you are in your thirties or forties . . . This is a very good time to transition to optician work because you will not spend too long in training and the salary is good enough for bringing in extra income. Retail opticians often have the option of working part-time, which can be an added incentive if you have family obligations.

If you are in your fifties . . . If you have good math and science facility and some experience with machinery and precision work, you will be especially welcomed at retail operations, after you have your diploma, because they can have high turnover and will be interested in someone who presents as reliable and steady who is willing to stay for a longer haul.

If you are over sixty . . . If you have experience with machinery and precision work, you will also be an attractive candidate at a retail operation.

*funded. I jumped at the chance to apply and I was accepted. I abso-
lutely loved it. After completing the program, I worked as an apprentice for three years at a local Pearle Vision. Then I passed my state
board exam (whew!) and was a full-fledged optician. This is almost 20
years ago now.*

What are the keys to success in this profession?

*I think the biggest key to success in my field is loving what you do. Every
person is different and has individual needs. Glasses are really very
personal, and are a part of someone's personality, something I always
strive to keep in mind with a client. Besides loving the work, you also
have to keep up with all the changes in the field. There are always new
advancements in lenses and frame styles—which is fun—and then there's
my least favorite part: insurance coverage.*

You should also consider getting a certificate to overcome any customer
or employer concerns that your age might mean you are less manually
adept or that you are less informed about the state of the art than someone younger.

Further Resources

ABO and NCLE   The American Board of Opticianry and the National
Contact Lens Examiners operate a joint Web site for opticians. Look here
for certifying information, continuing education, and media information. http://www.abo-ncle.org

Opticians Association of America   A national membership organization offering a job board, online educational opportunities, information
on state societies, a calendar of events, news, and current legislation information. http://www.oaa.org/index.shtml

Occupational Therapist

Occupational Therapist

Career Compasses

Guide yourself to a career as an occupational therapist.

Relevant Knowledge of occupational therapy techniques and equipment (40%)

Caring about your patients and their progress (20%)

Communication Skills to work effectively with patients, family members, employers, and colleagues (20%)

Organizational Skills to record patient progress and compare notes (20%)

Destination: Occupational Therapist

Similar to physical therapists, occupational therapists work with people whose abilities have been compromised to help them regain skills or learn adaptive techniques. Their patients have conditions that are either mentally, physically, developmentally, or emotionally disabling. An occupational therapist (OT) uses a number of treatments to help the patient either recover lost skills or develop abilities to cope with their condition. The focus ranges from simple improvement of motor functions or cognitive skills, to dealing with a permanent loss of ability. An OT seeks to guide his or her patient to a life as independent, productive, and satisfying as possible.

In the course of a day, OTs might work with someone who needs help in basic activities like dressing, cooking, and washing. They will also deal with people suffering cognitive problems that necessitate learning decision-making and problem-solving skills. They may have to help someone use a computer, or do physical therapy-style exercises geared toward improving strength and dexterity. Other exercises may involve improving memory or recognition or coordination.

Essential Gear

Back brace. You will probably do a lot of lifting and moving of patients and equipment, sometimes all day long. That, coupled with a lot of standing or driving, is hard on the body. Even if you are in great shape, you should still consider using a back brace to help you avoid injury.

When working with patients who have suffered injuries that have led to permanent disability or who have degenerative conditions such as muscular dystrophy, multiple sclerosis, or cerebral palsy, the OT conducts a number of therapies. These can range from teaching patients how to use assistive equipment such as wheelchairs, canes, orthoses (shoe inserts designed to support the foot), and aids for dressing and even eating. An OT might even design or build equipment to help with certain needs at home or in the workplace.

Many OT patients have developed conditions that create problems in their workplace. Whereas at one time, this would have forced them to change jobs or even stop working altogether, such circumstances can often be avoided with the help of a good occupational therapist. An OT can come to the patient's workplace and, with the cooperation of the employer, create modifications or help install adaptive equipment that can keep the patient working effectively at no productivity loss to the employer and important gain to society. An OT may also work with patients whose physical or mental conditions have previously kept them from even searching for employment. As clients approach the job market, the OT will assess their abilities and suggest jobs based on their findings, teach basic work activities, and be available to discuss a patient's condition with a prospective employer.

An occupational therapist works with individuals over a long term, making this an extremely gratifying job for people who like to get closely involved with patients and see progress over a period of months or even years. The ability to assess and record that progress is one of the most important aspects of an OT's job. It is vital that records be clear, detailed, and accurate. This is essential not only for the OT's evaluation purposes but also for such needs as insurance, billing, and discussion with other health care providers, family members, and employers.

Many occupational therapists choose to specialize. They can work exclusively in pediatrics, geriatrics, or with people suffering mental problems. They can specialize further by groups with a particular disability or condition. OTs who specialize in pediatrics might work in a school for children with special needs, where they evaluate individual children's abilities, develop therapies, modify classroom equipment, and assist children so that they can get involved in school activities. Depending on the needs of the school or the students, an OT might work with one or more child individually or conduct small learning sessions. They may do some work in tandem with the teacher or consult on an administrative committee.

Those who specialize in pediatrics can also focus on pre-school children from as young as infancy. Medical advances have helped more premature babies to survive, but they can be developmentally compromised. An occupational therapist can develop early intervention therapies that can assist with developmental skills such as listening, following directions, playing with others, dressing, eating, or grooming.

Geriatric specialties are also growing, as more and more of the population lives longer and people want to remain independent as long as possible. An OT can work with an older person to teach them adaptive skills for remaining in their home even if they have decreased strength or mobility. They can also go to a patient's home and assess it for possible hazards and make recommendations for rearrangements and equipment to assist certain functions.

An occupational therapist working with someone in a mental capacity helps people who are either mentally ill, developmentally challenged, or emotionally disturbed. They may also work with people struggling with addictions to alcohol or drugs or who have eating disorders or chronic depression. The job in these cases will entail developing and engaging in activities with the patients that help them learn coping skills.

Most occupational therapists work in rehabilitation centers. The space can be noisy because there usually are a few patients in the room at the same time, and a number of machines and devices that make noise. Occupational therapy can also be tiring because the job requires spending much of the day on your feet, or driving or taking public transportation through the day to provide onsite services in a home or workplace. OTs also run the risk of strain or injury due to lifting patients and equipment.

To become an occupational therapist, a candidate must complete a master's degree in occupational therapy, which can be earned full-time or, increasingly, part-time. You can also earn a doctoral degree, but the master's is the minimum requirement. Coursework includes physical, biological, and behavioral sciences, and the application of occupational therapy theory and skills. You must also undertake six months of supervised fieldwork. You must then obtain your license by passing a national certification exam. Some states will have their own individual exams that you must pass as well, particularly if you are a specialist. You will then be awarded the title "Occupational Therapist Registered" (OTR).

Successful occupational therapists are patient, trustworthy, warm, and as adaptive as the equipment and therapies they use with their clients. Occupational therapy allows you to work closely with individuals and help them markedly improve their lives.

You Are Here

Determine if you have the basics to be an occupational therapist.

Are you an excellent observer of minutiae? As anyone who has done gardening knows, progress can be very slow and almost imperceptible, although you do know it is taking place. With occupational therapy, a patient's progress can be very slow and sometimes stall for weeks at a time. It is not enough to notice obvious progress. You also have to be someone who can keenly observe the slightest improvement. Perhaps there is a millimeter of difference between how far a person could raise his or her arm one week versus the previous week. To the patient, that may be virtually meaningless, but you know it is important. Both you and the patient will do better when you see these changes.

Navigating the Terrain

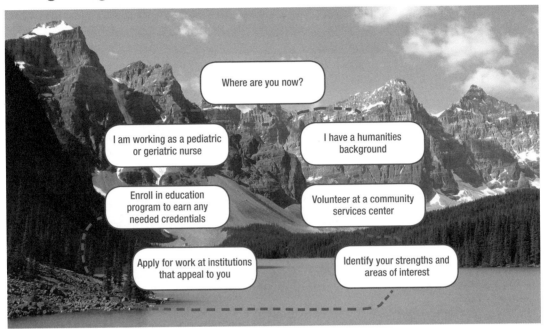

Where are you now?

I am working as a pediatric or geriatric nurse

I have a humanities background

Enroll in education program to earn any needed credentials

Volunteer at a community services center

Apply for work at institutions that appeal to you

Identify your strengths and areas of interest

Do you have endless stores of patience? Along these same lines, that slow progress can be immensely frustrating for both of you. This is especially true for someone who has enjoyed full health or mobility and is suddenly incapacitated. Patience and calm are required so you do not become aggravated by someone's lack of progress, even if he or she is hampering it by not engaging in home therapies or other recommended activities. You have to be someone who can encourage patients, guide them, and gently prod them where necessary. They have to have faith in the process, or there will be no improvement. It is your job to help them get and keep that faith, even when it looks almost hopeless.

Are you an inventive problem-solver? The therapies and activities developed by occupational therapists are done under strict guidelines, but because occupational therapy is a profession that helps individuals a lot of thought must still go into designing each treatment program. Whether finding a way for someone to adapt at work or at home, or helping someone with unusual cognitive dysfunctions, you must be

Notes from the Field

Audrey Zapletal
Occupational therapist, Thomas Jefferson University
Philadelphia, Pennsylvania

What were you doing before you got into occupational therapy?

I was working at a camp for kids with special needs, focusing on helping campers become more independent. And that's basically what occupational therapy is. It's all about helping people be independent. I'd originally applied for a different major but saw my mistake and changed in a week.

Why did you decide to pursue a career as an occupational therapist?

I was interested in work that involved helping people to find their abilities, no matter how small. What's wonderful with OT is that you can work with a wide range of people and needs, so you can help a parent learn to parent when their infant is in the neonatal ward, and then you can help a family cope when a relative has had a stroke. I wanted to look at people's strengths. I found it more motivating to use occupational therapy as a realm for treatment.

What was involved in terms of education/training and getting your first job?

It's a two- to three-year degree for an MS, or a five- to five-and-a-half year degree for the BS/MS. During your coursework, you get to observe fieldwork by going out with an occupational therapist and watching them

someone who enjoys thinking outside the box and finding unexpected and unique solutions to difficult problems.

Organizing Your Expedition

Prepare yourself to enter the world of occupational therapy.

Volunteer in a health care environment. You may have top-notch scientific aptitude and excellent problem-solving skills, and you may also be a great people person, but the hands-on work of occupational therapy work with a variety of patients. That's Level One fieldwork. In your last semester, you do Level Two fieldwork that involves two- to three-month rotations, working with an occupational therapist full time. They train you in a specialty and it varies per program. By the end of six months, you should be entry-level and ready to choose your specialty. They try to give you your first choice. I did three: adult rehab; skilled care; and acute care pediatrics. My absolute favorite was neonatal with pediatric outpatients. Before you actually begin work, you have to get your temporary license. Then you sit the national board exam to get your real license, but you can practice with the temporary license, so long as someone is supervising. I was in practice within three weeks of leaving the program.

What are the keys to success in occupational therapy?

You have to look at a person as a whole, and you have to discover who and what is important in that person's life. You have to be goal-oriented, because a lot of the work is about making goals for the patient and then working toward their achievement. You have to be someone who really enjoys a challenge. Occupational therapy school is very demanding. You have to be excellent with time management and communication because you are not just communicating with patients but with other team members. You have to learn constantly—the field is constantly growing, and you go to professional seminars regularly and come out with specific skills. Most of all, you have to absolutely love what you're doing. I love it so much I work seven days a week, but I don't consider it work.

requires something more. You need to be devoted, compassionate, and dedicated. Working with people who are ill, injured, frightened, and discouraged can be draining, but it can also be inspiring and invigorating, especially when you see that the work you are doing with them is having a positive effect. Seeing what a rehabilitation center or nursing home is really like will give you a sense of how you can handle it and what sort of work you will do on the job. And having that experience will make a big difference when you apply for the degree program, especially if you have not been otherwise involved in health care or do not have a science background.

Learn about other cultures and backgrounds. Whether going into a school, someone's workplace, or their home, you will find yourself dealing with a wide range of people, many of whom will be resistant to the idea of adaptive equipment or other changes, despite the medical necessities. The sort of therapies and exercises and activities entailed may be completely foreign to them and seem to go against a cultural grain. People can be fussy about the body. It is up to you to be understanding and sensitive to this. If you know something of their traditions and cultural practices, you can devise therapies that will feel more comfortable to certain patients. Remember that an enormous part of successful rehabilitation or adaptation is your personal relationship with patients. They must trust and like you. If they see that you have gone above and beyond to understand their situation and needs, that will help form a strong working relationship.

Essential Gear

Art classes. When working with developmentally challenged children or adults, a bit of art therapy can augment their other therapeutic activities. The patients may work with trained art therapists, but if you can work some art into the activities you arrange for them, it may be of use to both of you.

Consider learning another language. In addition to dealing with a wide range of people from various socioeconomic and cultural backgrounds, you may find yourself working with people for whom English is not their first language. This may not be as common for you as other health care professionals who work in free clinics, but again, the close nature of your relationship with your patients mean you do not want to have to rely on a translator for communications assistance. Additionally, you may want to work in speech-language therapy as part of your practice, and learning a language will give you added insight into the process of relearning or improving speech.

Learn some management skills. Many occupational therapists supervise aides and volunteers, as well as trainees. While strong interpersonal skills are probably most essential to the job, a good grasp of some basic management skills is useful too.

Landmarks

If you are in your twenties . . . If you have completed a BS in either biology or anatomy, or a BA in psychology, sociology, anthropology, or social sciences, you are a good candidate for the master's degree program. If you feel strongly about OT, you should also do some volunteer work in either OT itself, physical therapy, or in a nursing home to gain some good practical experience.

If you are in your thirties or forties . . . If you have some science or experience in working one-to-one with a wide range of people, you should research accredited degree programs and job opportunities in your area. If you have family obligations and need to go to school part-time, that is increasingly an option.

If you are in your fifties . . . If you are already in health care in some capacity, you may be able to apply some of your experience toward course credit. Consult with the advisor at your school of choice as to the possibility, although you should be prepared to have to take the full master's program.

If you are over sixty . . . If you have experience working with people who have some limitations, you may be very desirable in a pediatrics or school environment where they need someone who is enthusiastic and inventive, but can also exert a steadying presence.

Further Resources

The American Occupational Therapy Association A professional membership organization to promote and advance occupational therapy. It provides information about the work, education, continuing education opportunities, publications, and a job board. http://www.aota.org

State Occupational Therapy Associations Each individual state has its own OT association, providing information on accredited educational programs, licensing requirements, and job openings.

Genetic Counselor

Genetic Counselor

Career Compasses

Guide yourself to a career as a genetic counselor.

Relevant Knowledge of genetics, genetic disorders, and testing (40%)

Caring about the families with whom you work (25%)

Communication Skills to work effectively with the families and help them make decisions and take action (25%)

Ability to Manage Stress because you will deal with a lot of emotion and must be able to handle it without its affecting your work or demeanor (10%)

Destination: Genetic Counselor

A genetic counselor combines skills in psychology and counseling with a vast knowledge of genetics and science to be important members of health care teams assisting families as they process genetic information. The genetic counselor (GC) breaks down information in a comprehensible manner, so that families trying to have a baby or dealing with a disease can best understand their challenges and then take the necessary steps to move forward.

Knowledge is power, but as medical and scientific advances have done a great deal in recent years to unlock the code of the human genome, knowledge has also spawned concerns and even fears. As people learn more about their genetic dispositions and possibilities, they become worried about disease. A GC can explain what their genetic code really means and put into perspective their chances for developing a condition themselves or passing one onto a child. A GC teaches patients to recognize possible symptoms so that, if they do begin to manifest a disease or condition, it can be treated early. Clients, then, can also be more proactive about their health and health maintenance. Just because a woman is at high genetic risk for breast cancer does not mean she will actually develop the disease. However, knowing she is a high-risk prospect does mean that she must be vigilant about regular mammograms, scans, and self-checking for any breast changes. A good GC details findings but also helps people approach a situation as positively as is feasible, so that the science does not get overwhelmed by the emotions.

Essential Gear

Support network. Because classes are so small and the field still comparatively new, genetic counselors are a tight-knit group. Local organizations meet regularly to discuss new tests and other issues. More importantly, they are there for each other to help deal with some of the emotional stress of the job. While you have to try to keep your personal emotions out of the work, it will still be a drain. It is crucial that you have a strong support group to which you can take frustrations and worries and gain comfort and relief.

That said, an important part of the GC's job is helping people deal with news that can be emotionally upsetting. A GC not only gives a family information in a manner that is clear and comprehensible, they also offer support when a family discovers a member has a birth defect or genetic disorder. The GC is available not only for that support but also for questions, assistance, advocacy, and whatever else is needed during that difficult time. They also refer the family to long-term counselors, should that be required.

More generally, genetic counselors work with a medical team to determine if people are at risk for inherited conditions. They interpret the findings, do detailed histories so that they can draw a conclusive analysis of inheritance patterns and possible risks, and list the range of options, which they discuss with the family.

Genetic counselors also work as educators and resources for both the public and other health care professionals. Many are involved with genetic research as well. It is a varied job that is growing apace. The bulk of genetic counselors continue to work in the traditional area of prenatal counseling, but the other paths are expanding. Areas of specialty beyond prenatal include pediatric genetics, cancer genetics, adult genetics, neurogenetics, public health, and molecular/cytogenetic testing.

To become a genetic counselor, you must earn a master's degree from an accredited program of genetic counseling. As of 2008, there were 23 such programs in the country, although these are expected to grow. You should be aware, however, that the nature of the training is very intense, which means classes have to be small. Thus, competition to get into an accredited program is extremely stiff. Many aspiring genetic counselors have studied or have a bachelor's degree in psychology, biology, genetics, nursing, social work, or a similar field. Having some actual counseling experience is a definite plus. It is also recommended that you shadow a GC for a short while to get a feel of the work and assure yourself that this is something about which you feel passionate. If you cannot shadow a GC for some reason, you should certainly ask for some informational interviews with one or more. The master's degree program takes two years, and encompasses the summers as well. The coursework includes genetics, psychosocial theory, ethics, and counseling. You work in classrooms, labs, and under supervision in clinics, and you also prepare a research project. Once you have finished your coursework and have logged enough clinical hours (you must have 50 supervised cases), you are then eligible to take the American Board of Genetic Counseling's (ABGC) exams for certification. This is a fairly involved process, as you must first apply for "active candidate status" and then, once this has been granted, sit two exams. However, you can still get a job if you are of "active candidate status."

The competitive nature of the application process to get into an accredited program means that schools will be looking at the whole of your personality in addition to your science aptitude and experience. They want to see that you are calm, empathetic, and nonjudgmental. You should be understanding of different traditions and cultures and how those backgrounds are brought to bear on medical decisions. You must be able to advise without bringing your personal opinions into the fray. That said, you must also be pro-choice. Additionally, you must be an excellent observer. Much of your work involves asking questions and looking for information and then piecing together what you have in order to draw a useful conclusion. This sort of challenge should be exciting to you and one to which you look forward every day.

While the application process for schooling can be daunting, and the coursework and training rigorous, your chances of getting the job of your choice when you are certified are excellent. More and more people in health care and the public are recognizing the value of genetic counselors and calling upon their unique expertise to help guide them through complex and difficult decisions. It can be a draining job but one that is full of interesting challenges and satisfaction.

You Are Here

Determine if you have what it takes to be a genetic counselor.

Do you have a strong comprehension of medical information? Understanding intricate and involved scientific and medical information is crucial to being a good genetic counselor. Moreover, you must not only be able to understand sophisticated information but also be able to break it down in a manner patients understand. Your patients will come from a diverse socioeconomic range and have varying levels of education. You cannot make any assumptions about their comprehension, so you must be able to engage with them without condescension or lack of clarity. Basically, you have to be able to understand the science in plain English and then impart it in kind.

Are you observant? Much of your work is akin to solving mysteries. Patients do not always know pertinent information about their family histories, so you have to piece together data from what they do know, what their blood work indicates, and your own observations. There may be many hidden clues in their information, and you have to be able to ferret it out. Sometimes you will pick up on something unexpected, and you must then be ready to go a different tack and ask a series of different questions, or do additional research.

Can you work independently? While you are a member of a health care team and any number of colleagues will be available to advise or

Navigating the Terrain

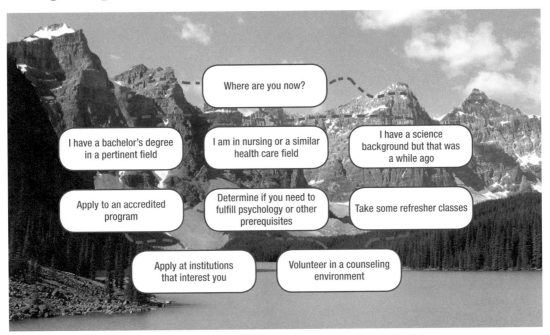

Where are you now?

I have a bachelor's degree in a pertinent field

I am in nursing or a similar health care field

I have a science background but that was a while ago

Apply to an accredited program

Determine if you need to fulfill psychology or other prerequisites

Take some refresher classes

Apply at institutions that interest you

Volunteer in a counseling environment

consult with you, you must also take on a lot of independent research. You will spend a lot of hours investigating the intricacies of genetic disorders. Also, the speed of medical developments means that there are always new tests to work with, and you must learn how to use them and interpret their results, as well as to understand the underlying science. You must be good with computers and devoted to getting to the bottom of a mystery on your own.

Organizing Your Expedition

Prepare yourself for entering the world of genetic counseling.

Meet with and ask to shadow genetic counselors. This is a requirement for application to a number of accredited programs, but it is also a good way to learn about the intricacies of the daily work before you begin. The majority of genetic counselors become interested in the work because they have done some study of science and psychology and want

Notes from the Field

Lindsey Campbell
Genetic counselor, Children's Hospital of Philadelphia
Philadelphia, Pennsylvania

What were you doing before you got into genetic counseling?

I knew I wanted to be in medicine in some way. My mother worked with kids who had genetic problems, which got me interested in genetics. I double majored in biology and psychology and just fell in love with my genetics classes. In my junior year at college, I had an internship studying cancer cells, which was interesting, but I knew I wanted to work with people. I'm a people person, and I really wanted a job where I could have personal interactions.

Why did you decide to pursue a career in genetic counseling?

It was something people came to from very mixed backgrounds, and it really spoke to me. It was a different approach to medicine. I hadn't realized I could combine my various interests and skills. I only wish it was more publicized. Everyone I know in the field seemed to have just stumbled upon it.

What sort of education/training was involved with getting your first job?

I did the master's degree at one of the accredited programs. There are only 23, but there will be more. Most of the classes are in psychology and biology with a lot of focus on duality [of gene-environment interactions] You get some real experience shadowing a genetic counselor and

to combine those interests. Many of them know they want to work in health care in some capacity, but are not interested in the traditional routes. In particular, they have a deep desire to work with people, but they want to be hands-on and involved, and have time to get to know people and really consult with them at length. They want to be able to do some good in people's lives and make a significant difference. All this is possible with genetic counseling, but the actual work, especially when one must break upsetting news, can be very difficult. The process of determining someone's genetic disorder can be complex and frustrating. It takes a very particular sort of person who can handle it with success. You want to be sure before you embark down this road that you are *slowly take on more responsibility. You train across all settings and then pick a specialty when you graduate. Then you have to get board, but you can work in your field before you're certified. You're called a "BC" (before certification). You can also switch your specialty if you want. I wanted to stay in Philadelphia. I'd done a rotation here and knew what I wanted and the job was available at Children's Hospital—it all kind of fell together.*

What are the keys to success in genetic counseling?

You have to be a good listener. That is huge. You really have to pay attention to how people might process information, and you have to notice how they ask questions. You also have to have the ability to communicate complex information to people with a variety of educational backgrounds and be sensitive to cultural values. You will approach everyone a bit differently, and you always have to be aware of ethical issues. You should really have a counseling background—this work should resonate with you. You have to have a combined interest in psychology, counseling, and science. You also need to be the type of person who can handle a lot of emotion. The work can be emotionally burdensome, and your psychology training will only do so much—you have to be able to take on people's problems and yet stay strong. We all get a bit overwhelmed sometimes, even though we got into this field because we want to help people. There's a really strong network of genetic counselors and we meet regularly to discuss issues—it's a very tight community.

that person and that the job is for you. Genetic counselors by nature are very warm, open, approachable people, and they love to talk about their work. If you have a genuine interest, capacity, and passion, the GC you are shadowing will want to help you, and may be happy to write one of your letters of recommendation.

Volunteer at a suicide hotline or Planned Parenthood. You come up against a wide range of issues, as well as emotional reactions, when working with people in genetic counseling. Some people will be angry and take that anger out on you. Some will be devastated, and want to cry on your shoulder. Many will be deeply conflicted or confused and want heartfelt advice and direction, and answers to dozens of questions. Besides shadowing a GC for a few days or week, you should get some hands-on experience working with people in a range of emotional states and needs. Learning to talk with people when they are frightened or distraught is invaluable to your success as a GC. Understanding how to help people see options and possibilities, even in what looks like a hopeless situation, will make you effective and give you greater personal satisfaction. By volunteering in such an environment, you will not only ascertain if you have the ability and personality to do the job well but whether you can then leave the job when you go home for the day and live your own life.

Essential Gear

Advocacy skills. Valuable research with stem cells is proceeding more slowly than it might because of political concerns, so that progress in combating some genetic disorders or cancers is impeded. A number of genetic counselors get involved in public policy to help people understand what is really involved in such research and try to persuade governments to let such research go forward.

Learn about different cultures. The intimate nature of genetic counseling can be very awkward and difficult for people whose background precludes that kind of discussion with a stranger. Likewise, when it comes time to impart information and make recommendations, you want to be aware of cultural antecedents and taboos that may create complications when attempting standard tests or operations. Understanding where people are coming from and how backgrounds can influence approaches to genetic counseling and action will help you in your interactions and help you make more appropriate recommendations.

Landmarks

If you are in your twenties . . . If you are a recent graduate in a pertinent field with a passionate interest in GC work, you should devote a year or so to either volunteering or doing paid work in some sort of counseling environment. Most applicants to the master's degree are young, but a level of experience is still looked for.

If you are in your thirties or forties . . . If you have some sort of counseling background, consult with the advisor at your chosen school as to your scientific aptitude and overall application chances. You may want to take some general science courses prior to applying.

If you are in your fifties . . . If you are in health care already, you should expect that your experience will help with your application, but will not count toward course credits. However, you should definitely consult with the advisor as to that possibility.

If you are over sixty . . . If you have a counseling background and strong science, you should not be swayed by the fact that most of the students are in their twenties. The field needs people with strong abilities and passion, and there are a number of students who have not even been in the workforce in years but are drawn to the unique opportunities of genetic counseling.

Further Resources

National Society of Genetic Counselors The NSGC is a membership organization that helps the public find a GC and also serves as a voice for genetic counselors. It offers education and career information, publications and news, and holds annual meetings. http://www.nsgc.org
American Board of Genetic Counseling The official credentialing organization for genetic counseling programs. You can consult the board for information on education programs and certification exams. There are also meetings, events, and consumer information. http://www.abgc.net

Appendix A

Going Solo: Starting Your Own Business

Starting your own business can be very rewarding—not only in terms of potential financial success, but also in the pleasure derived from building something from the ground up, contributing to the community, being your own boss, and feeling reasonably in control of your fate. However, business ownership carries its own obligations—both in terms of long hours of hard work and new financial and legal responsibilities. If you succeed in growing your business, your responsibilities only increase. Many new business owners come in expecting freedom only to find themselves chained tighter to their desks than ever before. Still, many business owners find greater satisfaction in their career paths than do workers employed by others.

The Internet has also changed the playing field for small business owners, making it easier than ever before to strike out on your own. While small mom-and-pop businesses such as hairdressers and grocery stores have always been part of the economic landscape, the Internet has made reaching and marketing to a niche easier and more profitable. This has made possible a boom in *microbusinesses*. Generally, a microbusiness is considered to have under ten employees. A microbusiness is also sometimes called a *SoHo* for "small office/home office."

The following appendix is intended to explain, in general terms, the steps in launching a small business, no matter whether it is selling your Web-design services or opening a pizzeria with business partners. It will also point out some of the things you will need to bear in mind. Remember also that the particular obligations of your municipality, state, province, or country may vary, and that this is by no means a substitute for doing your own legwork. Further suggested reading is listed at the end.

Crafting a Business Plan

It has often been said that success is 1 percent inspiration and 99 percent perspiration. However, the interface between the two can often be hard to achieve. The first step to taking your idea and making it reality is constructing a viable *business plan*. The purpose of a business plan is to think things all the way through, to make sure your ideas really are profitable, and to figure out the "who, what, when, where, why, and how" of your business. It fills in the details for three areas: your goals, why you think they are attainable, and how you plan to get to there. "You need to know where you're going before you take that first step," says Drew Curtis, successful Internet entrepreneur and founder of the popular newsfilter Fark.com.

Take care in writing your business plan. Generally, these documents contain several parts: An *executive summary* stating the essence of the plan; a *market summary* explaining how a need exists for the product and service you will supply and giving an idea of potential profitability by comparing your business to similar organizations; a *company description* which includes your products and services, why you think your organization will succeed, and any special advantages you have, as well as a description of *organization* and *management*; and your *marketing and sales strategy*. This last item should include market highlights and demographic information and trends that relate to your proposal. Also include a *funding request* for the amount of start-up capital you will need. This is supported by a section on *financials*, or the sort of cash flow you can expect, based on market analysis, projection, and comparison with existing companies. Other needed information, such as personal financial history, résumés, legal documents, or pictures of your product, can be placed in *appendices*.

Use your business plan to get an idea of how much startup money is necessary and to discipline your thinking and challenge your preconceived notions before you develop your cash flow. The business plan will tell you how long it will take before you turn a profit, which in turn is linked to how long it will before you will be able to pay back investors or a bank loan—which is something that anyone supplying you with money will want to know. Even if you are planning to subside on grants or you are not planning on investment or even starting a for-profit company, the discipline imposed by the business plan is still the first step to organizing your venture.

A business plan also gives you a realistic view of your personal financial obligations. How long can you afford to live without regular income? How are you going to afford medical insurance? When will your business begin turning a profit? How much of a profit? Will you need to reinvest your profits in the business, or can you begin living off of them? Proper planning is key to success in any venture.

A final note on business plans: Take into account realistic expected profit minus realistic costs. Many small business owners begin by underestimating start-ups and variable costs (such as electricity bills), and then underpricing their product. This effectively paints them into a corner from which it is hard to make a profit. Allow for realistic market conditions on both the supply and the demand side.

Partnering Up

You should think long and hard about the decision to go into business with a partner (or partners). Whereas other people can bring needed capital, expertise, and labor to a business, they can also be liabilities. The questions you need to ask yourself are:

☞ Will this person be a full and equal partner? In other words, are they able to carry their own weight? Make a full and fair assessment of your potential partner's personality. Going into business with someone who lacks a work ethic, or prefers giving directions to working in the trenches, can be a frustrating experience.

☞ What will they contribute to the business? For instance, a partner may bring in start-up money, facilities, or equipment. However, consider if this is enough of a reason to bring them on board. You may be able to get the same advantages in another way—for instance, renting a garage rather than working out of your partner's. Likewise, doubling skill sets does not always double productivity.

☞ Do they have any liabilities? For instance, if your prospective partner has declared bankruptcy in the past, this can hurt your collective venture's ability to get credit.

☞ Will the profits be able to sustain all the partners? Many start-up ventures do not turn profits immediately, and what little they do produce can be spread thin amongst many partners. Carefully work out the math.

Also bear in mind that going into business together can put a strain on even the best personal relationships. No matter whether it is family, friends, or strangers, keep everything very professional with written agreements regarding these investments. Get everything in writing, and be clear where obligations begin and end. "It's important to go into business with the right people," says Curtis. "If you don't—if it degrades into infighting and petty bickering—it can really go south quickly."

Incorporating. . . or Not

Think long and hard about incorporating. Starting a business often requires a fairly large—and risky—financial investment, which in turn exposes you to personal liability. Furthermore, as your business grows, so does your risk. Incorporating can help you shield yourself from this liability. However, it also has disadvantages.

To begin with, incorporating is not necessary for conducting professional transactions such as obtaining bank accounts and credit. You can do this as a sole proprietor, partnership, or simply by filing a DBA ("doing business as") statement with your local court (also known as "trading as" or an "assumed business name"). The DBA is an accounting entity that facilitates commerce and keeps your business' money separate from your own. However, the DBA does not shield you from responsibility if your business fails. It is entirely possible to ruin your credit, lose your house, and have your other assets seized in the unfortunate event of bankruptcy.

The purpose of incorporating is to shield yourself from personal financial liability. In case the worst happens, only the business' assets can be taken. However, this is not always the best solution. Check your local laws: Many states have laws that prevent a creditor from seizing a non-incorporated small business' assets in case of owner bankruptcy. If you are a corporation, however, the things you use to do business that are owned by the corporation—your office equipment, computers, restaurant refrigerators, and other essential equipment—may be seized by creditors, leaving you no way to work yourself out of debt. This is why it is imperative to consult with a lawyer.

There are other areas in which being a corporation can be an advantage, such as business insurance. Depending on your business needs, insurance can be for a variety of things: malpractice, against delivery failures or spoilage, or liability against defective products or accidents. Furthermore, it is easier to hire employees, obtain credit, and buy health insurance as an organization than as an individual. However, on the downside, corporations are subject to specific and strict laws concerning management and ownership. Again, you should consult with a knowledgeable legal expert.

Among the things you should discuss with your legal expert are the advantages and disadvantages of incorporating in your jurisdiction and which type of incorporation is best for you. The laws on liability and how much of your profit will be taken away in taxes vary widely by state and country. Generally, most small businesses owners opt for *limited liability companies* (LLCs), which gives them more control and a more flexible management structure. (Another possibility is a *limited liability partnership*, or *LLP*, which is especially useful for professionals such as doctors and lawyers.) Finally, there is the *corporation*, which is characterized by transferable ownerships shares, perpetual succession, and, of course, limited liability.

Most small businesses are sole proprietorships, partnerships, or privately-owned corporations. In the past, not many incorporated, since it was necessary to have multiple owners to start a corporation. However, this is changing, since it is now possible in many states for an individual to form a corporation. Note also that the form your business takes is usually not set in stone: A sole proprietorship or partnership can switch to become an LLC as it grows and the risks increase; furthermore, a successful LLC can raise capital by changing its structure to become a corporation and selling stock.

Legal Issues

Many other legal issues besides incorporating (or not) need to be addressed before you start your business. It is impossible to speak directly to every possible business need in this brief appendix, since regulations, licenses, and health and safety codes vary by industry and locality. A restaurant in Manhattan, for instance, has to deal not only with the usual issues such as health inspectors, the state liquor board, but obscure regulations such as New York City's cabaret laws, which prohibit dancing without a license in a place where alcohol is sold. An asbestos-abatement company, on the other hand, has a very different set of standards it has to abide by, including federal regulations. Researching applicable laws is part of starting up any business.

Part of being a wise business owner is knowing when you need help. There is software available for things like bookkeeping, business plans, and Web site creation, but generally, consulting with a knowledgeable professional—an accountant or a lawyer (or both)—is the smartest move. One of the most common mistakes is believing that just because you have expertise in the technical aspects of a certain field, you know all about running a business in that field. Whereas some people may balk at the expense, by suggesting the best way to deal with possible problems, as well as cutting through red tape and seeing possible pitfalls that you may not even have been aware of, such professionals usually more than make up for their cost. After all, they have far more experience at this than does a first-time business owner!

Financial

Another necessary first step in starting a business is obtaining a bank account. However, having the account is not as important as what you do with it. One of the most common problems with small businesses is undercapitalization—especially in brick-and-mortar businesses that sell or make something, rather than service-based businesses. The rule of thumb is that you should have access to money equal to your first year's anticipated profits, plus start-up expenses. (Note that this is not the same as having the money on hand—see the discussion on lines of credit, below.) For instance, if your annual rent, salaries, and equipment will cost $50,000 and you expect $25,000 worth of profit in your first year, you should have access to $75,000 worth of financing.

You need to decide what sort of financing you will need. Small business loans have both advantages and disadvantages. They can provide critical start-up credit, but in order to obtain one, your personal credit will need to be good, and you will, of course, have to pay them off with interest. In general, the more you and your partners put into the business yourselves, the more credit lenders will be willing to extend to you.

Equity can come from your own personal investment, either in cash or an equity loan on your home. You may also want to consider bringing on partners—at least limited financial partners—as a way to cover start-up costs.

It is also worth considering obtaining a line of credit instead of a loan. A loan is taken out all at once, but with a line of credit, you draw on the money as you need it. This both saves you interest payments and means that you have the money you need when you need it. Taking out too large of a loan can be worse than having no money at all! It just sits there collecting interest—or, worse, is spent on something utterly un-necessary—and then is not around when you need it most.

The first five years are the hardest for any business venture; your venture has about double the usual chance of closing in this time (1 out of 6, rather than 1 out of 12). You will probably have to tighten your belt at home, as well as work long hours and keep careful track of your business expenses. Be careful with your money. Do not take unnecessary risks, play it conservatively, and always keep some capital in reserve for emergencies. The hardest part of a new business, of course, is the learning curve of figuring out what, exactly, you need to do to make a profit, and so the best advice is to have plenty of savings—or a job to provide income—while you learn the ropes.

One thing you should not do is count on venture capitalists or "angel investors," that is, businesspeople who make a living investing on other businesses in the hopes that their equity in the company will increase in value. Venture capitalists have gotten something of a reputation as indiscriminate spendthrifts due to some poor choices made during the dot-com boom of the late 1990s, but the fact is that most do not take risks on unproven products. Rather, they are attracted to young companies that have the potential to become regional or national powerhouses and give better-than-average returns. Nor are venture capitalists are endless sources of money; rather, they are savvy businesspeople who are usually attracted to companies that have already experienced a measure of success. Therefore, it is better to rely on your own resources until you have proven your business will work.

Bookkeeping 101

The principles of double-entry bookkeeping have not changed much since its invention in the fifteenth century: one column records debits, and one records credits. The trick is *doing* it. As a small business owner, you need to be disciplined and meticulous at recording your finances. Thankfully, today there is software available that can do everything from tracking payables and receivables to running checks and generating reports.

Honestly ask yourself if you are the sort of person who does a good job keeping track of finances. If you are not, outsource to a bookkeeping company or hire someone to come in once or twice a week to enter invoices and generate checks for you. Also remember that if you have employees or even freelancers, you will have to file tax forms for them at the end of the year.

Another good idea is to have an accountant for your business to handle advice and taxes (federal, state, local, sales tax, etc.). In fact, consulting with an a certified public accountant is a good idea in general, since they are usually aware of laws and rules that you have never even heard of.

Finally, keep your personal and business accounting separate. If your business ever gets audited, the first thing the IRS looks for is personal expenses disguised as business expenses. A good accountant can help you to know what are legitimate business expenses. Everything you take from the business account, such as payroll and reimbursement, must be recorded and classified.

Being an Employer

Know your situation regarding employees. To begin with, if you have any employees, you will need an Employer Identification Number (EIN), also sometimes called a Federal Tax Identification Number. Getting an EIN is simple: You can fill out IRS form SS-4, or complete the process online at http://www.irs.gov.

Having employees carries other responsibilities and legalities with it. To begin with, you will need to pay payroll taxes (otherwise known as "withholding") to cover income tax, unemployment insurance, Social Security, and Medicare, as well as file W-2 and W-4 forms with the government. You will also be required to pay workman's compensation insurance, and will probably also want to find medical insurance. You are also required to abide by your state's nondiscrimination laws. Most states require you to post nondiscrimination and compensation notices in a public area.

Many employers are tempted to unofficially hire workers "off the books." This can have advantages, but can also mean entering a legal gray area. (Note, however, this is different from hiring freelancers, a temp employed by another company, or having a self-employed professional such as an accountant or bookkeeper come in occasionally to provide a service.) It is one thing to hire the neighbor's teenage son on a one-time basis to help you move some boxes, but quite another to have full-time workers working on a cash-and-carry basis. Regular wages must be noted in the accounts, and gaps may be questioned in the event of an audit. If the workers are injured on the job, you are not covered by workman's comp, and are thus vulnerable to lawsuits. If the workers you hired are not legal residents, you can also be liable for civil and criminal penalties. In general, it is best to keep your employees as above-board as possible.

Building a Business

Good business practices are essential to success. First off, do not overextend yourself. Be honest about what you can do and in what time frame. Secondly, be a responsible business owner. In general, if there is a problem, it is best to explain matters honestly to your clients than to leave them without word and wondering. In the former case, there is at least the possibility of salvaging your reputation and credibility.

Most business is still built by personal contacts and word of mouth. It is for this reason that maintaining your list of contacts is an essential practice. Even if a particular contact may not be useful at a particular moment, a future opportunity may present itself—or you may be able to send someone else to them. Networking, in other words, is as important when you are the boss as when you are looking for a job yourself. As the owner of a company, having a network means getting services on better terms, knowing where to go if you need help with a particular problem, or simply being in the right place at the right time to exploit an opportunity. Join professional organizations, the local Chamber of Commerce, clubs and community organizations, and learn to play golf. And remember—never burn a bridge.

Advertising is another way to build a business. Planning an ad campaign is not as difficult as you might think: You probably already know your media market and business community. The trick is applying it. Again, go with your instincts. If you never look twice at your local weekly, other people probably do not, either. If you are in a high-tourist area, though, local tourists maps might be a good way to leverage your marketing dollar. Ask other people in your area or market who have business similar to your own. Depending on your focus, you might want to consider everything from AM radio or local TV networks, to national trade publications, to hiring a PR firm for an all-out blitz. By thinking about these questions, you can spend your advertising dollars most effectively.

Nor should you underestimate the power of using the Internet to build your business. It is a very powerful tool for small businesses, potentially reaching vast numbers of people for relatively little outlay of money. Launching a Web site has become the modern equivalent of hanging out your shingle. Even if you are primarily a brick-and-mortar business, a Web presence can still be an invaluable tool—your store or offices will show up on Google searches, plus customers can find directions to visit you in person. Furthermore, the Internet offers the small-business owner many useful tools. Print and design services, order fulfillment, credit card processing, and networking—both personal and in terms of linking to other sites—are all available online. Web advertising can be useful, too, either by advertising on specialty sites that appeal to your audience, or by using services such as Google AdWords.

Amateurish print ads, TV commercials, and Web sites do not speak well of your business. Good media should be well-designed, well-edited, and well-put together. It need not, however, be expensive. Shop around and, again, use your network.

Flexibility is also important. "In general, a business must adapt to changing conditions, find new customers and find new products or services that customers need when the demand for their older products or services diminishes," says James Peck, a Long Island, New York, entrepreneur. In other words, if your original plan is not working out, or if demand falls, see if you can parlay your experience, skills, and physical plant into meeting other needs. People are not the only ones who can change their path in life; organizations can, too.

A Final Word

In business, as in other areas of life, the advice of more experienced people is essential. "I think it really takes three businesses until you know what you're doing," Drew Curtis confides. "I sure didn't know what I was doing the first time." Listen to what others have to say, no matter whether it is about your Web site or your business plan. One possible solution is seeking out a mentor, someone who has previously launched a successful venture in this field. In any case, before taking any step, ask as many people as many questions as you can. Good advice is invaluable.

Further Resources

American Independent Business Alliance
http://www.amiba.net

American Small Business League
http://www.asbl.com

IRS Small Business and Self-Employed One-Stop Resource
http://www.irs.gov/businesses/small/index.html

The Riley Guide: Steps in Starting Your Own Business
http://www.rileyguide.com/steps.html

Small Business Administration
http://www.sba.gov

Appendix B

Outfitting Yourself for Career Success

As you contemplate a career shift, the first component is to assess your interests. You need to figure out what makes you tick, since there is a far greater chance that you will enjoy and succeed in a career that taps into your passions, inclinations, natural abilities, and training. If you have a general idea of what your interests are, you at least know in which direction you want to travel. You may know you want to simply switch from one sort of nursing to another, or change your life entirely and pursue a dream you have always held. In this case, you can use a specific volume of The Field Guides to Finding a New Career to discover which position to target. If you are unsure of your direction you want to take, well, then the entire scope of the series is open to you! Browse through to see what appeals to you, and see if it matches with your experience and abilities.

The next step you should take is to make a list—do it once in writing—of the skills you have used in a position of responsibility that transfer to the field you are entering. People in charge of interviewing and hiring may well understand that the skills they are looking for in a new hire are used in other fields, but you must spell it out. Most job descriptions are partly a list of skills. Map your experience into that, and very early in your contacts with a prospective employer explicitly address how you acquired your relevant skills. Pick a relatively unimportant aspect of the job to be your ready answer for where you would look forward to learning within the organization, if this seems essentially correct. When you transfer into a field, softly acknowledge a weakness while relating your readiness to learn, but never lose sight of the value you offer both in your abilities and in the freshness of your perspective.

Energy and Experience

The second component in career-switching success is energy. When Jim Fulmer was 61, he found himself forced to close his piano-repair business. However, he was able to parlay his knowledge of music, pianos, and the musical instruments industry into another job as a sales representative for a large piano manufacturer, and quickly built up a clientele of musical-instrument retailers throughout the East Coast. Fulmer's experience highlights another essential lesson for career-changers: There are plenty of opportunities out there, but jobs will not come to you—especially the career-oriented, well-paying ones. You have to seek them out.

Jim Fulmer's case also illustrates another important point: Former training and experience can be a key to success. "Anyone who has to make a career change in any stage of life has to look at what skills they have acquired but may not be aware of," he says. After all, people can more easily change into careers similar to the ones they are leaving. Training and experience also let you enter with a greater level of seniority, provided you have the other necessary qualifications. For instance, a nurse who is already experienced with administering drugs and their benefits and drawbacks, and who is also graced with the personality and charisma to work with the public, can become a pharmaceutical company sales representative.

Unlock Your Network

The next step toward unlocking the perfect job is networking. The term may be overused, but the idea is as old as civilization. More than other animals, humans need one another. With the Internet and telephone, never in history has it been easier to form (or revive) these essential links. One does not have to gird oneself and attend reunion-type events (though for many this is a fine tactic)—but keep open to opportunities to meet people who may be friendly to you in your field. Ben Franklin understood the principal well—*Poor Richard's Almanac* is something of a treatise on the importance or cultivating what Franklin called "friendships" with benefactors. So follow in the steps of the founding fathers and make friends to get ahead. Remember: helping others feels good; it's often the receiving that gets a little tricky. If you know someone particularly well-connected in your field, consider tapping one or two less important connections first so that you make the most of the important one. As you proceed, keep your strengths foremost in your mind because the glue of commerce is mutual interest.

Eighty percent of job openings are *never advertised*, and, according to the U.S. Bureau of Labor statistics, more than half all employees landed their jobs through networking. Using your personal contacts is far more efficient and effective than trusting your résumé to the Web. On the Web, an employer needs to sort through tens of thousands—or millions—of résumés. When you direct your application to one potential employer, you are directing your inquiry to one person who already knows you. The personal touch is everything: Human beings are social animals, programmed to "read" body language; we are naturally inclined to trust those we meet in person, or who our friends and coworkers have recommended. While Web sites can be useful (for looking through help-wanted ads, for instance), expecting employers to pick you out of the slush pile is as effective as throwing your résumé into a black hole.

Do not send your résumé out just to make yourself feel like you're doing something. The proper way to go about things is to employ discipline and order, and then to apply your charm. Begin your networking efforts by making a list of people you can talk to: colleagues, coworkers, and supervisors, people you have had working relationship with, people from church, athletic teams, political organizations, or other community groups, friends, and relatives. You can expand your networking opportunities by following the suggestions in each chapter of the volumes. Your goal here is not so much to land a job as to expand your possibilities and knowledge: Though the people on your list may not be in the position to help you themselves, they might know someone who is. Meeting with them might also help you understand traits that matter and skills that are valued in the field in which you are interested. Even if the person is a potential employer, it is best to phrase your request as if you were seeking information: "You might not be able to help me, but do you know someone I could talk to who could tell me more about what it is like to work in this field?" Being hungry gives one impression, being desperate quite another.

Keep in mind that networking is a two-way street. If you meet someone who had an opening that is not right for you, but if you could recommend someone else, you have just added to your list two people who will be favorably disposed toward you in the future. Also, bear in mind that *you* can help people in *your* old field, thus adding to your own contacts list.

Networking is especially important to the self-employed or those who start their own businesses. Many people in this situation begin because they either recognize a potential market in a field that they are familiar with, or because full-time employment in this industry is no longer a possibility. Already being well-established in a field can help, but so can asking connections for potential work and generally making it known that you are ready, willing, and able to work. Working your professional connections, in many cases, is the *only* way to establish yourself. A free-lancer's network, in many cases, is like a spider's web. The spider casts out many strands, since he or she never knows which one might land the next meal.

Dial-Up Help

In general, it is better to call contacts directly than to e-mail them. E-mails are easy for busy people to ignore or overlook, even if they do not mean to. Explain your situation as briefly as possible (see the discussion of the "elevator speech"), and ask if you could meet briefly, either at their office or at a neutral place such as a café. (Be sure that you pay the bill in such a situation—it is a way of showing you appreciate their time and effort.) If you get someone's voicemail, give your "elevator speech" and then say you will call back in a few days to follow up—and then do so. If you reach your contact directly and they are too busy to speak or meet with you, make a definite appointment to call back at a later date. Be persistent, but not annoying.

Once you have arranged a meeting, prep yourself. Look at industry publications both in print and online, as well as news reports (here, GoogleNews, which lets you search through online news reports, can be very handy). Having up-to-date information on industry trends shows that you are dedicated, knowledgeable, and focused. Having specific questions on employers and requests for suggestions will set you apart from the rest of the job-hunting pack. Knowing the score—for instance, asking about the value of one sort of certification instead of another— pegs you as an "insider," rather than a dilettante, someone whose name is worth remembering and passing along to a potential employer.

Finally, set the right mood. Here, a little self-hypnosis goes a long way: Look at yourself in the mirror, and tell yourself that you are an enthusiastic, committed professional. Mood affects confidence and per-formance. Discipline your mind so you keep your perspective and self-respect. Nobody wants to hire someone who comes across as insincere, tells a sob story, or is still in the doldrums of having lost their previous job. At the end of any networking meeting, ask for someone else who might be able to help you in your journey to finding a position in this field, either with information or a potential job opening.

Get a Lift

When you meet with a contact in person (as well as when you run into anyone by chance who may be able to help you), you need an "elevator speech" (so-named because it should be short enough to be delivered during an elevator ride from a ground level to a high floor). This is a summary in which, in less than two minutes, you give them a clear impression of who you are, where you come from, your experience and goals, and why you are on the path you are on. The motto above Plato's Academy holds true: Know Thyself (this is where our Career Compasses and guides will help you). A long and rambling "elevator story" will get you nowhere. Furthermore, be positive: Neither a sad-sack story nor a tirade explaining how everything that went wrong in your old job is someone else's fault will get you anywhere. However, an honest explanation of a less-than-fortunate circumstance, such as a decline in business forcing an office closing, needing to change residence to a place where you are not qualified to work in order to further your spouse's career, or needing to work fewer hours in order to care for an ailing family member, is only honest.

An elevator speech should show 1) you know the business involved; 2) you know the company; 3) you are qualified (here, try to relate your education and work experience to the new situation); and 4) you are goal-oriented, dependable, and hardworking. Striking a balance is important; you want to sound eager, but not overeager. You also want to show a steady work experience, but not that you have been so narrowly focused that you cannot adjust. Most important is emphasizing what you can do for the company. You will be surprised how much information you can include in two minutes. Practice this speech in front of a mirror until you have the key points down perfectly. It should sound natural, and you should come across as friendly, confident, and assertive. Finally, remember eye contact! Good eye contact needs to be part of your presentation, as well as your everyday approach when meeting potential employers and leads.

Get Your Résumé Ready

Everyone knows what a résumé is, but how many of us have really thought about how to put one together? Perhaps no single part of the job search is subject to more anxiety—or myths and misunderstandings—than this 8 ½-by-11-inch sheet of paper.

On the one hand, it is perfectly all right for someone—especially in certain careers, such as academia—to have a résumé that is more than one page. On the other hand, you do not need to tell a future employer *everything*. Trim things down to the most relevant; for a 40-year-old to mention an internship from two decades ago is superfluous. Likewise, do not include irrelevant jobs, lest you seem like a professional career-changer.

Tailor your descriptions of your former employment to the particular position you are seeking. This is not to say you should lie, but do make your experience more appealing. If the job you're looking for involves supervising other people, say if you have done this in the past; if it involves specific knowledge or capabilities, mention that you possess these qualities. In general, try to make your past experience seem as similar to what you are seeking.

The standard advice is to put your Job Objective at the heading of the résumé. An alternative to this is a Professional Summary, which some recruiters and employers prefer. The difference is that a Job Objective mentions the position you are seeking, whereas a Professional Summary mentions your background (e.g. "Objective: To find a position as a sales representative in agribusiness machinery" versus "Experienced sales representative; strengths include background in agribusiness, as well as building team dynamics and market expansion"). Of course, it is easy to come up with two or three versions of the same document for different audiences.

The body of the résumé of an experienced worker varies a lot more than it does at the beginning of your career. You need not put your education or your job experience first; rather, your résumé should emphasize your strengths. If you have a master's degree in a related field, that might want to go before your unrelated job experience. Conversely, if too much education will harm you, you might want to bury that under the section on professional presentations you have given that show how good you are at communicating. If you are currently enrolled in a course or other professional development, be sure to note this (as well as your date of expected graduation). A résumé is a study of blurs, highlights, and jewels. You blur everything you must in order to fit the description of your experience to the job posting. You highlight what is relevant from each and any of your positions worth mentioning. The jewels are the little headers and such—craft them, since they are what is seen first.

You may also want to include professional organizations, work-related achievements, and special abilities, such as your fluency in a foreign language. Also mention your computer software qualifications and capabilities, especially if you are looking for work in a technological field or if you are an older job-seeker who might be perceived as behind the technology curve. Including your interests or family information might or might not be a good idea—no one really cares about your bridge club, and in fact they might worry that your marathon training might take away from your work commitments, but, on the other hand, mentioning your golf handicap or three children might be a good idea if your potential employer is an avid golfer or is a family woman herself.

You can either include your references or simply note, "References available upon request." However, be sure to ask your references' permission to use their names and alert them to the fact that they may be contacted before you include them on your résumé! Be sure to include name, organization, phone number, and e-mail address for each contact.

Today, word processors make it easy to format your résumé. However, beware of prepackaged résumé "wizards"—they do not make you stand out in the crowd. Feel free to strike out on your own, but remember the most important thing in formatting a résumé is consistency. Unless you have a background in typography, do not get too fancy. Finally, be sure to have someone (or several people!) read your résumé over for you.

For more information on résumé writing, check out Web sites such as http://www.resume.monster.com.

Craft Your Cover Letter

It is appropriate to include a cover letter with your résumé. A cover letter lets you convey extra information about yourself that does not fit or is not always appropriate in your résumé, such as why you are no longer working in your original field of employment. You can and should also mention the name of anyone who referred you to the job. You can go into some detail about the reason you are a great match, given the job description. Also address any questions that might be raised in the potential employer's mind (for instance, a gap in employment). Do not, however, ramble on. Your cover letter should stay focused on your goal: To offer a strong, positive impression of yourself and persuade the hiring manager that you are worth an interview. Your cover letter gives you a chance to stand out from the other applicants and sell yourself. In fact, according to a CareerBuilder.com survey, 23 percent of hiring managers say a candidate's ability to relate his or her experience to the job at hand is a top hiring consideration.

Even if you are not a great writer, you can still craft a positive yet concise cover letter in three paragraphs: An introduction containing the specifics of the job you are applying for; a summary of why you are a good fit for the position and what you can do for the company; and a closing with a request for an interview, contact information, and thanks. Remember to vary the structure and tone of your cover letter—do not begin every sentence with "I."

Ace Your Interview

In truth, your interview begins well before you arrive. Be sure to have read up well on the company and its industry. Use Web sites and magazines—http://www.hoovers.com offers free basic business information, and trade magazines deliver both information and a feel for the industries they cover. Also, do not neglect talking to people in your circle who might know about trends in the field. Leave enough time to digest the information so that you can give some independent thought to the company's history and prospects. You don't need to expert when you arrive to be interviewed; but you should be comfortable. The most important element of all is to be poised and relaxed during the interview itself. Preparation and practice can help a lot.

Be sure to develop well-thought-through answers to the following, typical interview openers and standard questsions.

☞ Tell me about yourself. (Do not complain about how unsatisfied you were in your former career, but give a brief summary of your applicable background and interest in the particular job area.) If there is a basis to it, emphasize how much you love to work and how you are a team player.

☞ Why do you want this job? (Speak from the brain, and the heart—of course you want the money, but say a little here about what you find interesting about the field and the company's role in it.)

☞ What makes you a good hire? (Remember here to connect the company's needs and your skill set. Ultimately, your selling points probably come down to one thing: you will make your employer money. You want the prospective hirer to see that your skills are valuable not to the world in general but to this specific company's bottom line. What can you do for them?)

☞ What led you to leave your last job? (If you were fired, still try say something positive, such as, "The business went through a challenging time, and some of the junior marketing people were let go.")

Practice answering these and other questions, and try to be genuinely positive about yourself, and patient with the process. Be secure but not cocky; don't be shy about forcing the focus now and then on positive contributions you have made in your working life—just be specific. As with the elevator speech, practice in front of the mirror.

A couple pleasantries are as natural a way as any to start the actual interview, but observe the interviewer closely for any cues to fall silent and formally begin. Answer directly; when in doubt, finish your phrase and look to the interviewer. Without taking command, you can always ask, "Is there more you would like to know?" Your attentiveness will convey respect. Let your personality show too—a positive attitude and a grounded sense of your abilities will go a long way to getting you considered. During the interview, keep your cell phone off and do not look at your watch. Toward the end of your meeting, you may be asked whether you have any questions. It is a good idea to have one or two in mind. A few examples follow:

☞ "What makes your company special in the field?"
☞ "What do you consider the hardest part of this position?"
☞ "Where are your greatest opportunities for growth?"
☞ "Do you know when you might need anything further from me?"

Leave discussion of terms for future conversations. Make a cordial, smooth exit.

Remember to Follow Up

Send a thank-you note. Employers surveyed by CareerBuilder.com in 2005 said it matters. About 15 percent said they would not hire someone who did not follow up with a thanks. And almost 33 percent would think less of a candidate. The form of the note does not much matter—if you know a manager's preference, use it. Otherwise, just be sure to follow up.

Winning an Offer

A job offer can feel like the culmination of a long and difficult struggle. So naturally, when you hear them, you may be tempted to jump at the offer. Don't. Once an employer wants you, he or she will usually give you a chance to consider the offer. This is the time to discuss terms of employment, such as vacation, overtime, and benefits. A little effort now can be well worth it in the future. Be sure to do a check of prevailing salaries for your field and area before signing on. Web sites for this include Payscale.com, Salary.com, and Salaryexpert.com. If you are thinking about asking for better or different terms from what the prospective employer offered, rest assured—that's how business gets done; and it may just burnish the positive impression you have already made.

Index

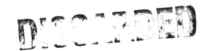